EMOTIONAL INTELLIGENCE

HOW TO MASTER SELF-AWARENESS, EMPATHY, AND SOCIAL SKILLS FOR DEEPER, MORE MEANINGFUL RELATIONSHIPS

MINDFULMINDS CO

© **Copyright 2024 - All rights reserved.**

The content of this book may not be reproduced, duplicated, or transmitted without the author's or the publisher's direct written permission.

Under no circumstances will any blame or legal responsibility be held against the publisher or author for any damages, reparation, or monetary loss due to the information contained within this book, either directly or indirectly.

Legal Notice:

This book is copyright-protected and only for personal use. You cannot amend, distribute, sell, use, quote, or paraphrase any part or content without the author's or publisher's consent.

Disclaimer Notice:

Please note the information in this document is for educational and entertainment purposes only. All efforts have been made to present accurate, up-to-date, reliable, and complete information. No warranties of any kind are declared or implied. Readers acknowledge that the author does not render legal, financial, medical, or professional advice. The content in this book has been derived from various sources. Please consult a licensed professional before attempting any techniques outlined in this book.

By reading this document, the reader agrees that the author is under no circumstances responsible for any direct or indirect losses incurred from using the information contained within this document, including, but not limited to, errors, omissions, or inaccuracies.

TABLE OF CONTENTS

Acknowledgments — 7
Introduction — 9

1. DEFINING EMOTIONAL INTELLIGENCE — 11
   1.1 The Birth of Emotional Intelligence: A Historical Overview — 11
   1.2 The Pillars of Emotional Intelligence: Self-Awareness, Regulation, and Empathy — 13
   1.3 Emotional Intelligence versus Intelligence Quotient: The Great Debate — 16
   1.4 The Role of Emotional Intelligence in Everyday Life — 18

2. THE IMPORTANCE OF EMOTIONAL INTELLIGENCE — 23
   2.1 Emotional Intelligence and Personal Success: A Strong Connection — 23
   2.2 The EQ Influence: Relationships, Work, and Happiness — 26
   2.3 How Emotional Intelligence Shapes Leaders — 28
   2.4 Emotional Intelligence: A Key Ingredient in Parenting — 31

3. CULTIVATING THE SEED OF EMOTIONAL INTELLIGENCE: SELF-AWARENESS — 35
   3.1 The Mirror of Self-Awareness: Reflection Techniques — 36
   3.2 Overcoming the Barriers to Self-Awareness — 39
   3.3 Implementing Emotional Self-Awareness in Daily Life — 41
   3.4 Case Study: Transformation Through Self-Awareness — 44

4. EMOTIONAL REGULATION: FIND YOUR BALANCE — 47
   4.1 Emotional Triggers: A Guide to Identification — 47
   4.2 Tools for Effective Emotional Regulation — 50

4.3 Overcoming Emotional Overwhelm: Steps to
Freedom ... 52
4.4 Snapshot: Achieving Balance Through Emotional
Regulation ... 54

5. EMPATHY: WALKING IN ANOTHER'S SHOES ... 59
5.1 Empathy versus Sympathy: A Crucial
Differentiation ... 60
5.2 Strategies to Enhance Empathy ... 62
5.3 Empathy in Action: Real-Life Scenarios ... 64
5.4 Personal Story: A Journey Toward Empathy ... 66

6. EMOTIONAL INTELLIGENCE: THE
INTERSECTION WITH MINDFULNESS ... 71
6.1 Understanding Mindfulness: A Basic Guide ... 72
6.2 Mindfulness Techniques for Enhanced
Emotional Intelligence ... 74
6.3 How Mindfulness Improves Emotional Response ... 77
6.4 Experience Report: Emotional Growth Through
Mindfulness ... 79

7. BUILDING RESILIENCE: THE EMOTIONAL
SHIELD ... 83
7.1 The Concept of Resilience: An Overview ... 83
7.2 Techniques to Foster Emotional Resilience ... 85
7.3 Resilience in the Face of Adversity: How to
Bounce Back ... 88
7.4 Resilience Triumph: A Real-Life Account ... 91

8. EMOTIONAL AGILITY: DANCE WITH YOUR
EMOTIONS ... 95
8.1 Emotional Agility Defined: The New Age
Concept ... 95
8.2 Strategies for Developing Emotional Agility ... 98
8.3 Emotional Agility at Work: A Practical Scenario ... 100
8.4 Emotional Agility Success Story: A Personal
Account ... 103

9. EMOTIONAL INTELLIGENCE FOR BETTER
RELATIONSHIPS ... 107
9.1 Relationship Dynamics: The Role of Emotional
Intelligence ... 108
9.2 Emotional Intelligence Techniques for
Harmonious Relationships ... 110

    9.3 Handling Difficult People with Emotional
    Intelligence   113
    9.4 Relationship Transformation: An Emotional
    Intelligence Success Story   115

10. **EMOTIONAL INTELLIGENCE: YOUR HIDDEN SUPERPOWER AT WORK**   119
    10.1 The Impact of Emotional Intelligence on Career Success   119
    10.2 Techniques to Apply Emotional Intelligence at Work   122
    10.3 Handling Workplace Stress with Emotional Intelligence   124
    10.4 Workplace Victory: An Emotional Intelligence Case Study   127

11. **EMOTIONAL INTELLIGENCE: NURTURING THE HEART OF PARENTING**   131
    11.1 The Importance of Emotional Intelligence in Parenting   132
    11.2 Emotional Intelligence Techniques for Effective Parenting   134
    11.3 Teaching Kids Emotional Intelligence: Practical Tips   137
    11.4 Parenting Success: An Emotional Intelligence Journey   139

12. **EMOTIONAL INTELLIGENCE: A BEACON OF LIGHT IN MENTAL HEALTH**   143
    12.1 The Interplay Between Emotional Intelligence and Mental Health   144
    12.2 Using Emotional Intelligence to Manage Anxiety and Depression   146
    12.3 Emotional Intelligence for Improved Psychological Well-Being   148
    12.4 Triumph Over Mental Health Challenges: An Emotional Intelligence Story   151

Conclusion   155
References   159

EMOTIONAL INTELLIGENCE QUIZ
TAKE THE QUIZ BEFORE READING

Welcome to a journey of self-discovery and emotional growth. Before diving into the rich content of this book on emotional intelligence, I invite you to explore an essential tool designed to enhance your reading experience: the Emotional Intelligence Quiz.

Emotions are the heartbeat of our existence, influencing every aspect of our lives. Understanding them can unlock a world of insight and well-being. This quiz is a thoughtfully crafted starting point, offering you a personalized snapshot of your emotional landscape. By participating in the quiz, you will gain valuable insights into your emotional strengths and areas for growth, setting the stage for a more meaningful and transformative journey through the book.

Imagine reading with a deeper awareness of your emotional tendencies, equipped with knowledge that makes each chapter resonate on a personal level. The quiz is not just a preliminary step but a key that unlocks a more profound understanding of the concepts you are about to explore. It will prepare you to engage more fully with the material, enriching your journey towards greater emotional intelligence.

Take a moment now to complete the quiz by scanning the QR code. Embrace this opportunity to reflect on your emotions and prime your mind for the enlightening journey ahead. Your path to emotional mastery begins here.

ACKNOWLEDGMENTS

Emotional Intelligence would not be what it is without a circle of invaluable support.

Thank you to my family and friends for their unwavering support and encouragement through every step of this process.

A special thanks goes to the MindfulMinds Co. team for their guidance and expertise in shaping this book.

I'm immensely grateful to my editors at Publishing Services for their meticulous attention to detail and dedication to making this manuscript the best it could be.

My mentors deserve a heartfelt acknowledgment for their wisdom and insights that have deeply influenced this work.

And, of course, a big thank you to you, the reader. Your curiosity and willingness to learn about emotional intelligence have made all this effort meaningful.

Thank you to everyone who has contributed to this journey. Your support has been pivotal in bringing this book to life.

INTRODUCTION

Emotions play a pivotal role in the maze of human existence. They are the driving force behind our actions, reactions, relationships, and, ultimately, our well-being. My journey of understanding and managing emotions has been transformative, and I have realized emotions' profound power over our lives.

This book is the outcome of my exploration into emotional intelligence. It is the first step we will undertake together to comprehend and navigate the complex landscape of our feelings. I invite you to join me as we explore the fascinating world of emotions and emotional intelligence.

Emotions are subjective experiences, as we all know. However, they are far from unscientific. Research has shown there is a neurological basis for every emotion we experience. An intriguing fact is that our brain has a structure known as the amygdala, which acts as an emotional processing hub. It's involved in the appraisal and regulation of emotions, thereby playing a critical role in our emotional responses.

The goal of this book is not merely to provide information or share scientific facts. It is to offer a vision—a vision of a life where emotions are not our masters but our allies. We will learn to understand our emotions, not fear them. We will learn to manage our emotions, not suppress them. We will learn to use our emotions to enhance our relationships, decision-making, and overall well-being.

As we embark on this journey, I want you to remember that mastering emotions is not about achieving perfection. It's about progress. It's about developing the capacity to recognize, understand, and manage our feelings effectively. It's about cultivating emotional intelligence.

Throughout this book, I will share insights from my experiences, exercises to practice, and recommendations to help you build emotional intelligence. By the end of the journey, I hope you will gain the tools to decode your emotions, stop overthinking, and lead a happier, more fulfilled life.

DEFINING EMOTIONAL INTELLIGENCE

1.1 THE BIRTH OF EMOTIONAL INTELLIGENCE: A HISTORICAL OVERVIEW

The concept of emotional intelligence, often abbreviated as EI or EQ (emotional quotient), is not as recent as one might assume. Though its popularization occurred in the last few decades, its roots extend much deeper into the annals of psychological research.

The seed was planted in the 1930s when Edward Thorndike, an American psychologist, introduced the idea of "social intelligence"—the ability to understand and navigate social situations and relationships. This idea marked the first significant deviation from the traditional and narrow understanding of intelligence, which focused primarily on cognitive abilities, such as logical reasoning and problem-solving.

Fast forward to the 1980s, psychologists began exploring the dimensions of intelligence beyond the cognitive. Howard Gardner's theory of multiple intelligences reframed our understanding of intelligence. He proposed that intelligence is not a single, static IQ score but rather a dynamic array of different types of intelligence, including interpersonal and intrapersonal intelligence. These two types of intelligence closely resemble what we now understand as emotional intelligence.

However, the term "emotional intelligence" was not formally introduced until 1990 when psychologists Peter Salovey and John D. Mayer developed a model that defined it as the ability to recognize, understand, manage, and use emotions in oneself and others. For the first time, emotions were seen as by-products of our experiences and integral components of our intelligence that could be harnessed and utilized.

Emotional intelligence truly came to the forefront of public consciousness in 1995, when science journalist Daniel Goleman published his groundbreaking book, *Emotional Intelligence: Why It Can Matter More Than IQ*. Goleman expanded on Salovey and Mayer's model and proposed that EQ was a more significant determinant of success and well-being than traditional intelligence measured by IQ. His book sparked a revolution, not just in psychological circles but in businesses, schools, and homes worldwide.

Over time, the concept of emotional intelligence has evolved and been refined. Despite the different models and definitions, its essence remains consistent: it's about recognizing, understanding, managing, and effectively using emotions in ourselves and others.

Let's consider a practical scenario to illustrate this. Suppose you're in a team meeting at work, and tension is rising over a disagreement about a project. An emotionally intelligent person would recognize and manage their increasing frustration and notice the subtle signs of distress in others—clenched jaws, impatient foot tapping, and avoiding eye contact. They would then use this understanding to navigate the situation, perhaps by suggesting a short break or calmly expressing their viewpoint and encouraging others to do the same. They would use their emotions as tools rather than being controlled by them.

Today, emotional intelligence is widely recognized as a crucial skill in personal and professional life. It is taught in schools, implemented in corporate training programs, and sought after in potential leaders. Yet, despite its widespread recognition and application, many of us struggle to truly understand and apply emotional intelligence in our everyday lives. This book aims to bridge this gap, providing a practical guide to understanding and developing emotional intelligence.

As we delve deeper into the subsequent chapters, we will explore the various components of emotional intelligence (EQ), learn how to enhance our own EQ and discover how to apply these skills in real-life situations. We will uncover the path to understanding and mastering our emotions.

1.2 THE PILLARS OF EMOTIONAL INTELLIGENCE: SELF-AWARENESS, REGULATION, AND EMPATHY

Emotional Intelligence, as a construct, is multifaceted. We must comprehend its foundational pillars to grasp its depth and richness. These pillars, or components, include self-awareness, self-regulation, and empathy. Each plays a vital role in shaping our emotional landscape and contributes to our overall emotional intelligence.

Understanding Self-Awareness: Recognizing and Understanding Personal Moods and Emotions

The first pillar of emotional intelligence is self-awareness. It forms the bedrock upon which other components rest. Self-awareness pertains to our ability to identify and understand our emotions and moods. It's about tuning into our internal emotional states and recognizing how they influence our thoughts and behaviors.

Imagine being in a situation where you're feeling unusually irritable but can't figure out why. You snap at a colleague for a minor mistake and regret it later. This situation points to a lack of self-awareness. You might have managed your response better if you recognized your irritability and its possible cause.

To develop self-awareness, we need to cultivate a habit of introspection, observing our emotions without judgment. Mindfulness, a form of meditation focused on the present moment, can be a valuable tool. It enables us to monitor our emotional state in real-time, recognizing when we're feeling anxious, excited, frustrated, or calm.

Embracing Self-Regulation: Managing Impulses, Maintaining Integrity, and Taking Responsibility

The second pillar of emotional intelligence is self-regulation. Once we can recognize and understand our emotions through self-awareness, the next step is to manage them effectively. Self-regulation is all about our ability to control our emotional responses instead of letting our emotions control us.

Consider a situation where you're stuck in traffic, making you late for an important meeting. The natural response might be to honk impatiently or lash out at other drivers. But with self-regulation, you could choose to remain calm, listen to some soothing music, or use the time to mentally prepare for the meeting. Here, you're controlling your emotional response rather than letting the situation dictate it.

Self-regulation also involves maintaining integrity and taking responsibility for our actions. It's about aligning our behaviors with our values, even in emotionally charged situations. In the workplace, this could mean admitting a mistake instead of blaming others or resisting the urge to gossip about a colleague.

The Power of Empathy: Recognizing and Understanding the Emotions of Others

The third pillar of emotional intelligence is empathy. While self-awareness and self-regulation focus on our own emotions, empathy involves tuning into the emotions of others. It's about understanding and responding to other people's feelings with care and respect.

Think about a time when a friend shared a problem with you. Did you rush to provide advice or listen attentively, trying to understand their feelings and perspectives? The latter response illustrates empathy. It's not about fixing others' problems; it's about understanding their emotional experience and showing that you care.

Empathy is a critical skill in building strong, meaningful relationships. It allows us to connect with others on a deeper level, fostering mutual understanding and respect. Whether in the family, workplace, or social circle, empathy can transform our interactions and relationships.

In the subsequent chapters, we will delve deeper into these pillars, exploring their significance, practical application, and strategies to enhance them. We will also consider how these pillars interact with each other and contribute to our overall emotional intelligence. By understanding and strengthening these pillars, we can build a robust foundation of emotional intelligence, equipping us to navigate our emotional world with greater ease and effectiveness.

1.3 EMOTIONAL INTELLIGENCE VERSUS INTELLIGENCE QUOTIENT: THE GREAT DEBATE

The world of psychology has been a battleground for the long-standing debate between emotional intelligence (EQ) and intelligence quotient (IQ). For many years, the spotlight was focused solely on IQ, a numerical measure of a person's reasoning ability. It was seen as the ultimate marker of intelligence, a predictor of academic achievement, professional success, and societal status.

IQ tests, developed in the early 20th century, primarily measure cognitive abilities like logic, abstract reasoning, learning ability, and problem-solving capacity. They have been used extensively in educational and professional settings to assess an individual's intelligence level relative to others in the same age group. The premise was simple: The higher your IQ, the more intelligent you were considered to be.

However, this traditional view of intelligence started to shift toward the end of the 20th century. The emergence of emotional intelligence offered a new perspective, challenging the supremacy of IQ. EQ brought emotions into the equation, highlighting their role in our overall intelligence. How we manage our feelings, understand others' emotions, and interact with people could be just as important, if not more, than our ability to solve complex problems or absorb new information.

This new view ushered in a new era in the understanding of intelligence, sparking what came to be known as the EQ versus IQ debate. The crux of this debate revolved around a central question: Which is a better predictor of success, EQ or IQ?

To answer this question, let's consider an example. Imagine two individuals, John and Mary. John has an above-average IQ, excels in solving complex mathematical problems, and has an impressive memory; however, he struggles with managing his emotions and often finds it difficult to understand others' feelings. On the other hand, Mary has an average IQ but a high EQ. She is adept at understanding and managing her emotions, empathizes with others, and has excellent social skills.

In the traditional view, John, with his higher IQ, would be considered more likely to succeed. However, Mary's high EQ could give her a significant edge in real-world scenarios. Her ability to understand and manage emotions could enable her to navigate the complexities of interpersonal relationships, work effectively in teams, and remain calm under pressure, all of which are crucial for success in many areas of life.

This does not imply that IQ is irrelevant. Cognitive abilities are undoubtedly important. They help us process information, solve problems, make decisions, and perform many cognitive tasks. However, EQ brings a different set of skills to the table—those related to our emotions and interactions with others. These skills are critical in many situations where cognitive abilities alone might fall short.

Emotional and cognitive intelligence are not mutually exclusive but complementary facets of our overall intelligence. They intersect and interact in complex ways that contribute to our behavior, decision-making, and overall well-being. For instance, our ability to regulate emotions (an aspect of EQ) can influence our decision-making capacity (associated with IQ) and vice versa.

As we move forward, we will explore these facets of emotional intelligence in greater detail, unraveling their intricacies and interconnectedness. We will learn how to enhance our EQ, augmenting not just our ability to understand and manage emotions but also our capacity to make decisions, solve problems, and navigate the complexities of life, thereby complementing and augmenting our IQ.

In this transformative exploration, we will discover that the real power lies not in choosing between EQ and IQ but in integrating both, creating a harmonious blend of cognitive and emotional intelligence. This integrated approach forms the basis for a balanced, fulfilling, and successful life, whether in personal relationships, professional endeavors, or individual well-being.

With this understanding, let's move forward to unravel the role of emotional intelligence in various aspects of our everyday lives. As we do so, remember that the goal is not to pit EQ against IQ but to understand how we can harness both to live a more balanced, successful, and fulfilling life.

1.4 THE ROLE OF EMOTIONAL INTELLIGENCE IN EVERYDAY LIFE

Emotional Intelligence in Personal Relationships

Navigating the nuances of personal relationships is a complex task. The dynamics are fluid and influenced by many factors; emotional intelligence is significant among these. It acts as the rudder that steers the ship of our relationships, guiding us through the choppy waters of emotional undercurrents and leading us toward the shore of harmony and mutual understanding.

Consider a disagreement with a loved one. Such situations are often emotionally charged and can lead to impulsive reactions. However, with a high EQ, you can recognize your rising frustration, regulate your emotional response, and empathize with the other person's perspective. Instead of lashing out, you can express your feelings calmly and listen to the other person's viewpoint, leading to a constructive conversation rather than a heated argument.

Emotional intelligence also enhances our ability to connect with others. It allows us to understand what a person says, feels, needs, and values. This deep emotional understanding fosters trust, mutual respect, and intimacy, forming the foundation of strong, fulfilling relationships.

The Impact of Emotional Intelligence in the Workplace

The professional sphere is another area where emotional intelligence plays a critical role. In the workplace, we interact with diverse individuals, each with unique personalities, emotions, and viewpoints. Emotional intelligence equips us to navigate these interactions effectively, fostering a positive, collaborative work environment.

Delays and conflicts are not uncommon in team settings. However, an emotionally intelligent team member can recognize the mounting tension, regulate their own emotional response, and empathize with the differing viewpoints. They can facilitate open, respectful communication, turning potential conflicts into opportunities for creative problem-solving and team growth.

Leaders with high EQ are particularly effective in motivating their teams. They can understand their team members' emotions, needs, and motivations and use this understanding to inspire and guide them toward their goals. Furthermore, they can manage their emotions effectively, remain calm under pressure, and make well-thought-out decisions, setting a positive example for their team.

The Influence of Emotional Intelligence on Mental Health

Our mental health is intricately linked with our emotions. Understanding, expressing, and managing our emotions can significantly influence our mental well-being. Emotional intelligence, with its focus on emotional awareness, regulation, and empathy, serves as a protective shield, safeguarding our mental health.

Take the example of dealing with stress. Life often throws stressful situations our way, and these can take a toll on our mental health if not managed effectively. However, with a high EQ, you can recognize the signs of stress early on, such as tension in your body, irritability, or difficulty concentrating. You can then use effective stress management techniques, such as deep breathing, mindfulness, or positive self-talk, to regulate your emotional response and mitigate the impact of stress on your mental health.

Emotional intelligence also aids in overcoming negative emotions, such as anxiety or depression. By understanding and accepting these emotions, we can manage them more effectively rather than suppressing or avoiding them. Furthermore, empathy, a key component of EQ, can help us feel understood and less alone in our struggles, fostering emotional resilience and well-being.

In essence, emotional intelligence acts as a compass, guiding us through the labyrinth of our emotional world. It helps us build fulfilling relationships, succeed in our professional endeavors, and safeguard our mental health. Its influence permeates every aspect of our lives, quietly steering us toward emotional balance and well-being. Understanding and enhancing our EQ allows us to navigate our emotional world more easily and effectively, leading to a more balanced, fulfilling, and successful life.

With this understanding of the foundational aspects of emotional intelligence, you're now ready to delve deeper into each of these components. In the following chapters, we will explore the pillars of emotional intelligence—self-awareness, self-regulation, and empathy—in greater detail. You will learn practical strategies to enhance these skills and discover how to apply them in various aspects of your life. As you continue reading, remember that the goal is not perfection but progress. Every step you take toward enhancing your EQ is a step toward a more emotionally balanced, fulfilling, and successful life.

THE IMPORTANCE OF EMOTIONAL INTELLIGENCE

Imagine standing at the edge of a serene lake on a calm day. As you cast a stone into the water, ripples begin to form, extending outwards from the point of impact. The stone, though small, profoundly affects the water's surface. This imagery is akin to the influence of emotional intelligence in our lives. Just as the stone creates ripples in the water, emotional intelligence (EI) has far-reaching effects on various aspects of our lives, ranging from personal growth and success to resilience in the face of adversity.

2.1 EMOTIONAL INTELLIGENCE AND PERSONAL SUCCESS: A STRONG CONNECTION

Personal growth and success stem from various factors, and emotional intelligence is a significant contributor. It's the invisible hand that subtly yet powerfully influences our choices, actions, and interactions.

How Emotional Intelligence Contributes to Personal Growth

One of the most compelling aspects of emotional intelligence is its ability to foster personal growth. Like a compass, it guides us through the complex terrain of our inner emotional world. Enhancing our self-awareness and emotional intelligence enables us to better understand our motivations, values, strengths, and areas for improvement. We become more attuned to our emotional responses and their triggers, which helps manage our reactions better.

For instance, suppose you've been experiencing a series of unproductive days. You're unsure about the cause until you dig deeper into your emotions. You realize that your lack of productivity is tied to feelings of overwhelm stemming from an overloaded work schedule. This self-awareness, a key component of emotional intelligence, allows you to take appropriate steps such as delegating tasks, prioritizing your to-do list, or setting boundaries on your work time, thereby enhancing your productivity.

The Role of Emotional Intelligence in Achieving Goals

Achievement of personal and professional goals is closely tied to personal growth. Emotional intelligence plays a critical role here. It aids in setting realistic goals, persisting in the face of obstacles, and managing stress and negative emotions that might arise in pursuing these goals.

Imagine you're preparing for a crucial presentation at work. As the day approaches, you start feeling anxious. Without emotional intelligence, you might let the anxiety consume you, affecting your performance. However, with a high EI, you recognize your anxiety and its source. You then use relaxation techniques to manage your anxiety and visualize a successful presentation to boost your confidence. You've used your emotional intelligence to manage your emotions, enabling you to perform at your best.

Emotional Intelligence and Resilience in the Face of Adversity

Life is not always a smooth sail. We often encounter storms of adversity and challenges. During these times, emotional intelligence shines as a beacon of resilience. Helping us understand and manage our emotions equips us to cope with stressful situations and bounce back from setbacks.

Consider a situation where you've faced a significant setback in your career, such as a missed promotion or job loss. An emotionally intelligent response would involve acknowledging your disappointment while also reminding yourself of your skills and past accomplishments. Instead of letting the setback define you, you view it as a temporary hurdle and an opportunity for growth. You then channel your energy into learning from the experience and planning your next steps. Your emotional intelligence has equipped you to deal with the setback resiliently.

Emotional intelligence, therefore, plays an integral role in personal growth, goal achievement, and resilience. Enhancing our emotional intelligence allows us to navigate our personal and professional lives more effectively, paving the way for personal success.

2.2 THE EQ INFLUENCE: RELATIONSHIPS, WORK, AND HAPPINESS

Emotional Intelligence in Building and Maintaining Relationships

In the vast tapestry of human interaction, relationships are the threads that bind us together. Emotional intelligence, focusing on emotional understanding and management, is akin to the needle that expertly weaves these threads, creating a strong, harmonious pattern.

Consider your interactions with a close friend. There are moments of joy, shared laughter, and common interests. Yet, there are also times of disagreement, misunderstandings, or hurt feelings. Emotional intelligence is what enables you to navigate these varied emotional landscapes. You can perceive your friend's unspoken feelings mirrored in their body language or tone of voice. You empathize with their experiences, creating a bond of mutual understanding. When conflicts arise, you manage your emotions, preventing heated responses and fostering constructive dialogue.

Moreover, emotional intelligence enhances your capacity for deep, genuine connections. By understanding your emotions, you express your feelings authentically, encouraging others to do the same. This emotional authenticity acts as the glue that bonds relationships, fostering trust and intimacy.

The Role of Emotional Intelligence in Career Advancement

The corridors of professional success are often lined with the milestones of emotional intelligence. Emotional intelligence is not just about technical expertise or hard skills; it's about managing your emotions, interacting with colleagues, and handling workplace challenges.

Take a moment to reflect on your workplace. It's a dynamic environment teeming with diverse personalities, tight deadlines, and high-stakes decisions. Navigating this environment requires more than just intellectual prowess—it requires emotional intelligence.

With a high EQ, you can manage work-related stress, preventing burnout and enhancing productivity. You can empathize with your colleagues, fostering collaborative relationships and teamwork. When faced with difficult decisions, you can make balanced, rational decisions instead of being swayed by strong emotions.

Moreover, emotional intelligence fuels career growth. As you climb the professional ladder, technical skills often take a backseat, and emotional intelligence comes to the forefront. Leaders with high emotional intelligence can motivate their teams, manage conflicts, and drive performance, thereby paving the path for career advancement.

How Emotional Intelligence Contributes to Overall Happiness

The pursuit of happiness is a universal human endeavor, and emotional intelligence serves as a reliable compass in this pursuit. The connection between emotional intelligence and happiness is akin to a well-choreographed dance, where each step and move is intricately linked.

Imagine going through your day. You wake up in the morning, engage with family members, go to work, interact with colleagues, face challenges, and enjoy accomplishments. Each of these instances involves emotions. Emotional intelligence allows you to navigate these daily instances in a manner that enhances your happiness.

By understanding and managing your emotions, you can shift your focus from negative to positive emotions, fostering a positive outlook. You can deal with life's ups and downs resiliently, preventing temporary setbacks from dampening your happiness. You can build fulfilling relationships, which significantly contribute to overall happiness.

Moreover, emotional intelligence allows you to find joy in the present moment instead of constantly chasing future goals. By being aware of your present emotions, you can savor positive experiences and manage negative ones effectively, thereby enhancing your day-to-day happiness.

In essence, emotional intelligence acts as a key that unlocks the door to fulfilling relationships, professional success, and overall happiness. Enhancing our emotional intelligence allows us to open this door and enter a life of greater harmony, success, and well-being.

2.3 HOW EMOTIONAL INTELLIGENCE SHAPES LEADERS

Leadership is multifaceted, involving a delicate balance of strategic planning, decision-making, team building, and conflict resolution. It's akin to conducting an orchestra, where diverse instruments must be harmoniously orchestrated to create a captivating symphony. In this orchestration, emotional intelligence serves as the conductor's baton, guiding the leader in effectively managing their emotions and those of their team members.

Emotional Intelligence in Decision-Making

Decisions are the lifeblood of leadership. From strategic planning to problem-solving, leaders continually make decisions that significantly impact their team and organization. Emotional intelligence is the lens that sharpens their decision-making prowess, enabling them to consider both logical and emotional aspects.

Imagine a leader facing a tough decision, such as downsizing the team due to budget cuts. Without emotional intelligence, the leader might focus solely on the financial aspect, overlooking the emotional impact on the team. However, with a high EQ, the leader can empathize with the team's potential anxieties, communicate the decision empathetically, and provide necessary support.

Furthermore, emotional intelligence aids self-regulation, preventing impulsive decisions fueled by strong emotions such as anger or frustration. It allows leaders to pause, reflect upon their emotional state, and make balanced, rational decisions.

The Role of Emotional Intelligence in Team Management

Teams are the backbone of any organization, and effective team management is vital to leadership. Emotional intelligence infuses empathy and emotional understanding into the leader's management style, fostering a positive, collaborative team environment.

Consider a situation where a team member is consistently missing deadlines. A leader with high emotional intelligence would not hastily reprimand the individual. They would instead seek to understand the reasons behind the behavior. It could be personal issues, workload stress, or lack of motivation. By understanding the individual's emotional state, the leader can provide the necessary support, such as workload adjustment, offering emotional support, or providing motivation, thereby enhancing the individual's performance and overall team productivity.

Moreover, leaders with high emotional intelligence foster emotional expression within the team, promoting open communication and mutual respect. They create a safe space where team members can express their thoughts and emotions without fear of judgment, leading to improved team cohesion and collaboration.

Emotional Intelligence and Conflict Resolution in Leadership

Conflicts are an inevitable part of any workplace. However, they can lead to creative solutions and strengthened relationships when handled effectively. Emotional intelligence is the leader's compass in navigating these conflicts, transforming potential discord into harmony.

Imagine a scenario where two team members disagree over a project approach. The conflict is escalating, affecting the team's morale. A leader with high emotional intelligence would recognize the rising tension and step in to mediate. They would listen empathetically to both parties, understand their viewpoints and emotions, and guide them toward a mutually agreeable solution. They would use the conflict as an opportunity for team growth rather than a source of discord.

Moreover, emotional intelligence equips leaders to manage their emotions during conflicts. Instead of reacting impulsively or taking sides, they can maintain composure, facilitating a balanced, fair resolution. This emotionally intelligent approach to conflict resolution fosters trust, respect, and collaboration within the team.

In the grand orchestra of leadership, emotional intelligence serves as the maestro's baton, guiding the leader in harmoniously conducting diverse decision-making instruments, team management, and conflict resolution. By enhancing their emotional intelligence, leaders can create a captivating symphony of productivity, collaboration, and team growth. It is the unseen force that subtly yet powerfully influences a leader's effectiveness, shaping them into a conductor of success and harmony.

2.4 EMOTIONAL INTELLIGENCE: A KEY INGREDIENT IN PARENTING

Fostering Emotional Intelligence in Children

In the world of parenting, the cultivation of emotional intelligence in children serves as a vital foundation for their emotional well-being, social relationships, and overall development. It is akin to planting a seed, nurturing it with the right amount of sunlight and water, and watching it grow into a sturdy tree.

One of the first steps toward fostering emotional intelligence in children involves helping them recognize and name their emotions. This can be done through simple activities such as discussing characters in a storybook or a movie and talking about their feelings. For instance, you could ask your child how they think a specific character felt when they lost their toy or won a race.

Emotional role-playing games can also be a fun and effective way to enhance children's emotional intelligence. You could use puppets, dolls, or even yourselves to enact different scenarios and talk about the emotions involved. This helps children understand various emotions and teaches them that expressing their feelings is okay.

The Role of Emotional Intelligence in Effective Communication with Children

Communication is the lifeline of any relationship, and parenting is no exception. Emotional intelligence, with its focus on emotional understanding and empathy, enhances the quality of communication with children, paving the way for stronger parent-child relationships.

An emotionally intelligent approach to communication involves actively listening to your child's feelings and responding with empathy. Instead of dismissing their fears about the first day of school as "silly," you acknowledge their feelings, saying something like, "I can see that you're worried about your first day. It's natural to feel this way when we're about to try something new."

This type of empathetic response validates the child's feelings, showing them that their feelings are important and understood. It fosters a sense of emotional safety and encourages the child to express their feelings openly.

How Emotional Intelligence Can Help in Managing Parenting Stress

While rewarding, parenting can often be a roller-coaster ride of joys, challenges, and stress. Emotional intelligence serves as a calming influence, helping parents manage their stress and navigate the parenting journey with greater ease.

One of the ways emotional intelligence aids in stress management is by enhancing self-awareness. By being aware of your emotional state, you can recognize signs of stress early on, such as irritability or exhaustion. This awareness allows you to take proactive steps to manage your stress, such as taking a break, practicing mindfulness, or seeking support.

Emotional Intelligence also equips you with the ability to regulate your emotions effectively. For instance, if your child's constant nagging triggers frustration, you can manage your response instead of reacting impulsively. You could take a few deep breaths, remind yourself that your child is just seeking attention, and respond calmly.

Moreover, empathy, a key component of emotional intelligence, helps you understand your child's behavior from their perspective, reducing feelings of stress or frustration. For instance, understanding that your toddler is throwing tantrums not to annoy you but because they're struggling to express their needs can help you respond with patience and understanding.

In essence, emotional intelligence plays a pivotal role in parenting. It fosters emotional intelligence in children, enhances communication, and manages parenting stress. Enhancing our emotional intelligence allows us to navigate the parenting journey with greater confidence, patience, and understanding, nurturing emotionally healthy and happy children.

As we bid adieu to this chapter, we carry forward the understanding of the profound influence of emotional intelligence in our lives. As our exploration continues in the subsequent chapters, let's prepare to delve deeper into the pillars of emotional intelligence, starting with self-awareness. Let's enter the fascinating world of self-discovery, understanding, and emotional balance.

CULTIVATING THE SEED OF EMOTIONAL INTELLIGENCE: SELF-AWARENESS

Imagine standing before a mirror. What do you see? Your reflection, of course. But look closer. Can you see the emotions that lie beneath the surface, subtly shaping your expressions? This is the essence of self-awareness, the first pillar of emotional intelligence. It's about looking into the mirror of your emotions, understanding what they tell you, and how they influence your thoughts and behaviors.

Self-awareness is the starting point of our emotional intelligence journey. Like a compass, it guides us through our internal emotional landscape, helping us understand where we are, where we're headed, and how we feel along the way. It's about being present with our emotions, acknowledging them without judgment, and using this understanding to navigate our lives more effectively.

3.1 THE MIRROR OF SELF-AWARENESS: REFLECTION TECHNIQUES

Developing self-awareness involves cultivating a habit of introspection, a regular practice of looking inward to understand our emotions. Here are some reflection techniques that can help you enhance your self-awareness.

Journaling for Emotional Clarity

Journaling is a powerful tool for self-reflection. It's like having a conversation with yourself, providing an outlet to express your thoughts and emotions freely. Here's how you can use journaling to enhance your self-awareness:

1. Create a regular journaling routine. Whether it's first thing in the morning, during your lunch break, or before bed, find a time that works for you and commit to journaling regularly. It needn't be lengthy—a few minutes each day can be enough to make a difference.
2. Write freely and honestly. Let your thoughts flow onto the page without censoring or judging them. Remember, this journal is for your eyes only. It's a safe space to express your feelings openly and honestly.
3. Reflect on your emotions. Don't just write about what happened during the day—write about how it made you feel. Did a conversation with a colleague leave you feeling frustrated? Did a friend's compliment make you feel happy and appreciated? Write it all down.
4. Look for patterns. Over time, you might notice patterns in your emotional responses. Perhaps you often feel anxious on Sunday evenings at the thought of the upcoming workweek, or maybe you notice a mood lift when you

spend time outdoors. Recognizing these patterns can provide valuable insights into your emotional triggers and patterns.

Mindfulness Meditation

Mindfulness meditation is another effective tool for enhancing self-awareness. It involves focusing on the present moment without judgment, helping you develop a heightened awareness of your emotional state.

Here's a simple mindfulness meditation technique you can try:

1. Find a quiet, comfortable place to sit. You can sit on a chair, on the floor, or anywhere you feel comfortable. The key is to maintain a posture that is relaxed yet alert.
2. Focus on your breath. Close your eyes and bring your attention to your breathing. Notice the sensation of the breath entering and leaving your body. If your mind wanders, gently bring it back to your breath.
3. Observe your emotions. As you continue to focus on your breath, turn your attention to your emotions. What are you feeling? Try to name the emotion—sadness, anger, joy, anxiety. Observe this emotion without trying to change it or judge it.
4. Practice regularly. As with any skill, practice is key. Aim for a few minutes of mindfulness meditation each day, gradually increasing the duration as you become more comfortable with the practice.

Emotional Check-Ins Throughout the Day

Conducting regular emotional check-ins is another effective way to enhance self-awareness. It's like taking your emotional temperature by gauging how you feel at different points throughout the day.

Here's how you can practice emotional check-ins:

1. Set reminders. Schedule a few regular times each day for your emotional check-ins. These could be during your morning coffee break, lunchtime, or evening before dinner.
2. Pause and reflect. When it's time for your check-in, take a moment to pause and tune into your feelings. Are you feeling energized or tired? Calm or stressed? Happy or sad? Try to identify your primary emotion at that moment.
3. Record your emotions. Jotting down your feelings in a notebook or an app might be helpful. This can help you track your emotional patterns over time, providing deeper insights into your emotional landscape.

By incorporating these reflection techniques into your daily routine, you can enhance your self-awareness and gain a clearer understanding of your emotions and how they influence your thoughts and behaviors. This understanding is the first step toward mastering your emotions, setting the stage for the development of other components of emotional intelligence.

3.2 OVERCOMING THE BARRIERS TO SELF-AWARENESS

Identifying Emotional Blind Spots

Just as a driver checks their vehicle's blind spots before changing lanes, we must also identify and understand our emotional blind spots to enhance self-awareness. Emotional blind spots are areas in our emotional landscape that remain hidden from our conscious awareness. They could be recurring emotional reactions, patterns of behavior, or biases that we fail to recognize in ourselves that can significantly impact our interactions and relationships.

For instance, you might often feel irritated when a colleague offers unsolicited advice without realizing your irritation stems from an underlying emotional blind spot related to a need for autonomy. Recognizing such blind spots can provide valuable insights into our emotions and behaviors, enabling us to manage them more effectively.

One way to identify emotional blind spots is through self-reflection. Reflect on situations where your emotional response was intense or seemed disproportionate to the problem. Could an underlying emotional blind spot be triggering this response? Consider patterns in your relationships or recurring issues at work. Could an unrecognized emotional blind spot be contributing to these patterns?

Challenging Cognitive Distortions

Cognitive distortions, also known as thinking errors, are another barrier to self-awareness. These irrational or exaggerated thought patterns can distort our perception of reality, trigger negative emotions, and hinder our self-awareness.

Some common cognitive distortions include "all-or-nothing" thinking (viewing things in black-and-white categories), "overgeneralization" (drawing broad conclusions from a single event), and "catastrophizing" (expecting the worst-case scenario).

For example, if you make a mistake in a work project and start thinking, "I always mess things up. I'm terrible at my job," you're falling into the trap of overgeneralization. This cognitive distortion can trigger feelings of inadequacy and failure, hindering self-awareness and emotional balance.

Challenging cognitive distortions involves recognizing these distorted thought patterns, questioning their validity, and replacing them with more rational and balanced thoughts. Cognitive behavioral therapy (CBT) techniques, such as thought records or cognitive restructuring, can be particularly effective in challenging cognitive distortions.

Seeking Feedback from Trusted Others

While self-reflection is crucial for self-awareness, we can also gain valuable insights into our emotions and behaviors by seeking feedback from others. Others can often see aspects of ourselves that we might overlook, providing a more complete picture of our emotional landscape.

Think of someone in your life who knows you well and whose opinion you value. It could be a close friend, a family member, a mentor, or a trusted colleague. Share with them your desire to enhance your self-awareness and ask for their honest feedback. Ask them about patterns they've noticed in your emotional responses, behaviors, or interactions. Remember to approach their feedback with an open mind and a willingness to learn and grow.

However, while feedback from others can be valuable, it's also important to remember that their perceptions are influenced by their own experiences and biases. Use their feedback as a guide, not as an absolute truth. Ultimately, self-awareness involves integrating both our self-perceptions and the feedback from others to gain a holistic understanding of our emotional selves.

By identifying emotional blind spots, challenging cognitive distortions, and seeking feedback from trusted others, we can overcome the barriers to self-awareness, paving the way for a deeper understanding of our emotions and heightened emotional intelligence. As we continue to develop our self-awareness, we prepare ourselves to explore the next pillar of emotional intelligence—emotional regulation—equipped with a clearer understanding of our emotional selves.

3.3 IMPLEMENTING EMOTIONAL SELF-AWARENESS IN DAILY LIFE

Acquiring knowledge about self-awareness is one thing, but the real magic happens when we apply this knowledge in our everyday lives. Let's explore how we can integrate self-awareness practices into our daily routine, making them a natural part of our lives.

Incorporating Mindfulness into Routine Activities

Mindfulness is the practice of being fully present in the moment, observing our thoughts, feelings, and sensations without judgment. It's a powerful tool for enhancing self-awareness. But how do we incorporate mindfulness into our daily activities?

The key lies in simplicity. We don't need to set aside a separate "mindfulness hour"—instead, we can infuse mindfulness into the activities we already do.

Consider your morning routine. As you brush your teeth or sip your coffee, focus on the present moment instead of letting your mind wander to the day's tasks. Pay attention to the coffee's taste, the toothbrush's sensation against your teeth, and the sound of the birds outside your window. This practice of mindful attention can serve as a 'check-in' with your emotional state, enhancing your self-awareness.

Similarly, during your workday, take short mindfulness breaks. Instead of scrolling through social media or thinking about your next task, take a few moments to just "be." Pay attention to your breath, your body, your emotions. These short breaks can help you reconnect with your emotional state, allowing you to manage your emotions more effectively.

Regular Self-Reflection Sessions

Self-reflection is another powerful tool for enhancing self-awareness. It involves taking time out of your day to reflect on your thoughts, feelings, and experiences. But how can we make self-reflection a regular part of our lives?

One way is to dedicate a specific time each day for self-reflection. It could be in the morning, when your mind is fresh, or at night when you're winding down from the day. During this time, reflect on your emotions throughout the day. What emotions did you experience? How did they influence your behavior? What might have triggered these emotions?

As you reflect, avoid judging your emotions or yourself. Remember, all emotions, whether positive or negative, are part of the human experience. The goal of self-reflection is not to criticize yourself but to understand your emotions and their impact on your life.

Using Emotion Tracking Apps

Technology can be a valuable ally in enhancing self-awareness in this digital age. Emotion-tracking apps are a testament to this. These apps provide a platform to record emotions and help you track your emotional patterns over time.

By consistently logging your emotions, you can start noticing patterns in your responses. For example, you might notice that you often feel stressed on Sunday evenings or that your mood lifts when you spend time in nature. These insights can help you better understand your emotional triggers and patterns, enhancing your self-awareness.

Remember, the aim of these apps is not to achieve a specific emotional state but to better understand your emotions. So, whether you're feeling joyful, anxious, excited, or sad, record it in the app. Over time, these entries will paint a picture of your emotional landscape, helping you navigate it with greater ease and understanding.

Integrating self-awareness into our daily lives might seem challenging at first. But with consistent practice, these techniques can become second nature, enhancing our emotional intelligence and paving the way for a more balanced, fulfilling life. Whether through mindfulness, self-reflection, or emotion-tracking apps, every step toward self-awareness brings us closer to understanding and mastering our emotions.

3.4 CASE STUDY: TRANSFORMATION THROUGH SELF-AWARENESS

Transformation is a powerful word. It speaks of change, growth, and evolution. Today, we will explore a real-life transformation brought about by the power of self-awareness. This is the story of Jane.

Jane's Path: From Emotional Ignorance to Self-Awareness

Jane, a successful marketing professional, was known for her excellent problem-solving skills and strategic thinking. However, she was often at a loss when it came to her emotions. She struggled to identify her feelings, frequently mistaking anxiety for anger or disappointment for sadness. This lack of emotional clarity, reflected in her personal and professional relationships, led to misunderstandings and conflicts.

Jane's lack of self-awareness wasn't uncommon. Many of us, like Jane, go through life unaware of our emotional selves. We react impulsively, fail to understand our triggers and struggle to manage our emotional responses. But Jane's story took a turn.

A Pivotal Moment: A Crisis Sparks Change

The change came in the form of a crisis. Jane's mother was diagnosed with a severe illness. As she navigated the complex world of healthcare, insurance, and caregiving, Jane found herself on an emotional roller-coaster. She experienced a wide range of emotions—fear, anxiety, sadness, frustration, and occasionally, moments of hope and joy.

This crisis served as a wake-up call. Jane realized that to navigate this challenging phase, she needed to understand her emotions better. She started reading about emotional intelligence and was introduced to the concept of self-awareness. Intrigued, Jane decided to put it into practice.

The Outcome: Enhanced Relationships and Personal Satisfaction

Jane started with small, simple steps. She began journaling, jotting down her thoughts and feelings each day. She practiced mindfulness, focusing on her breath and observing her emotions without judgment. She tried to identify and challenge her cognitive distortions, replacing irrational thoughts with balanced ones.

The transformation didn't happen overnight. There were days when Jane felt overwhelmed and doubted the effectiveness of these practices. But she persevered, motivated by the small yet significant changes she started observing in herself.

As Jane's self-awareness increased, she began to understand her emotions better. She could now differentiate between anxiety and anger, disappointment and sadness. She started recognizing her triggers, allowing her to manage her emotional responses effectively.

This newfound self-awareness profoundly impacted Jane's relationships. She could now communicate her feelings more clearly, reducing misunderstandings and conflicts. Jane became more empathetic at work, understanding her colleagues' perspectives and responding to them with emotional intelligence. At home, despite the ongoing crisis, Jane was able to provide emotional support to her family, managing her emotions and helping her family manage theirs.

Jane's story is a testament to the transformative power of self-awareness. It shows how enhancing our self-awareness can lead to better emotional management, improved relationships, and greater personal satisfaction.

Life will always have its ups, downs, joys, and sorrows. But with self-awareness, we can navigate this emotional roller-coaster with greater ease and resilience. We can understand our emotions, manage them effectively, and use them as a guide in our journey toward a balanced, fulfilling life.

As we close this chapter, let's carry forward the insights from Jane's transformation. Let's commit to cultivating self-awareness, understanding its power, and incorporating it into our daily lives. By doing so, we prepare ourselves to explore the next pillar of emotional intelligence—self-regulation—equipped with a clearer understanding of our emotional selves.

EMOTIONAL REGULATION: FIND YOUR BALANCE

Imagine standing on a tightrope. To your left is an abyss of chaos, and to your right, a chasm of rigidity. You are striving to stay centered, maintaining a delicate equilibrium. This balancing act is akin to emotional regulation, the second pillar of emotional intelligence. It's about maintaining emotional balance, neither suppressing our feelings nor allowing them to overpower us.

As we explore emotional regulation, we will uncover strategies to identify emotional triggers, tools to manage our emotional responses, and ways to overcome emotional overwhelm. Our exploration begins with a critical aspect of emotional regulation—identifying emotional triggers.

4.1 EMOTIONAL TRIGGERS: A GUIDE TO IDENTIFICATION

Emotional triggers are events, situations, or behaviors that evoke a strong emotional response in us. These triggers can vary widely from person to person, depending on their personal experiences, values, and beliefs. Recognizing our emotional triggers is the first step toward effective emotional regulation.

Recognizing Common Emotional Triggers

Common emotional triggers can range from specific situations or behaviors to certain words or tones of voice. For instance, a person might feel anxious when faced with a public speaking engagement or become angry when they feel criticized or judged.

Other common triggers might include feeling ignored, facing a significant change, or experiencing a personal setback. Even certain environmental factors, like a crowded room or a noisy environment, can act as triggers for some individuals.

Recognizing these triggers requires careful self-observation. Pay attention to situations or behaviors that often evoke a strong emotional response. Do you find yourself feeling anxious during team meetings at work? Do you often feel angry when your partner gives you constructive feedback? Noticing these patterns can help you identify your emotional triggers.

Personal Trigger Mapping

Personal trigger mapping is a useful technique for identifying emotional triggers. It involves creating a visual or written "map" of situations, behaviors, or experiences that trigger strong emotional responses in you.

To create a personal trigger map, start by listing your most common emotional responses, such as anger, anxiety, sadness, or frustration. For each emotion, note down the situations or behaviors that often trigger this emotion in you.

For instance, under "Anxiety," you might list triggers such as public speaking, meeting new people, or making important decisions. Under "Anger," you might include triggers such as feeling disrespected, facing injustice, or being interrupted.

Creating a personal trigger map can provide valuable insights into your emotional landscape, helping you better understand and manage your emotional responses.

The Role of Past Experiences in Trigger Formation

Our past experiences play a significant role in the formation of emotional triggers. Often, our triggers are linked to past events or experiences that were emotionally charged or traumatic.

For example, if you were bullied in school, you might feel triggered by behaviors that remind you of those bullying experiences, such as being teased or criticized. If you grew up in a household where anger was frequently expressed, you might be particularly sensitive to others' expressions of anger.

Reflecting on our past experiences can help us better understand our emotional triggers. It's not about dwelling on the past but understanding its influence on our present emotional responses. This understanding can provide a valuable context for our triggers, aiding in effective emotional regulation.

Identifying emotional triggers is a crucial aspect of emotional regulation. By recognizing our triggers, we better understand our emotional responses, empowering us to manage our emotions more effectively. As we continue our exploration of emotional regulation, we will build on this understanding, uncovering strategies and tools to manage our emotional responses effectively.

4.2 TOOLS FOR EFFECTIVE EMOTIONAL REGULATION

Successfully managing the ebb and flow of our emotions is like a skilled sailor deftly handling his ship amid the sea's undulating waves. A sailor uses various tools and techniques to keep the vessel steady, and similarly, we can employ a range of strategies to regulate our emotions effectively. Let's explore three powerful tools for emotional regulation: deep breathing exercises, cognitive reframing techniques, and progressive muscle relaxation.

Deep Breathing Exercises

Breathing, though an automatic bodily function, is a potent tool for emotional regulation. Deep breathing exercises can help us calm our minds, reduce stress, and effectively manage emotional responses.

One such exercise is the 4-7-8 technique, also known as the relaxing breath exercise. Here's how to do it:

1. Exhale completely through your mouth.
2. Close your mouth and inhale quietly through your nose to a mental count of four.
3. Hold your breath for a count of seven.
4. Exhale completely through your mouth to a count of eight.

This completes one breath. Repeat this cycle for four breaths. The 4-7-8 deep breathing exercise helps reduce anxiety, control stress, and calm the mind, enabling us to manage our emotional responses more effectively.

Cognitive Reframing Techniques

Cognitive reframing is a psychological technique that involves changing how we view situations, experiences, or events to better manage our emotional responses. It's about shifting our perspective to see the glass as half full rather than half empty.

For instance, suppose you're feeling stressed about a big presentation at work. A negative thought might be, "I'm going to mess up, and everyone will think I'm incompetent." Reframe this thought to "This presentation is a great opportunity for me to showcase my skills and learn from the experience."

By changing the narrative, we can manage our emotional responses to situations, experiences, or events more effectively. Cognitive reframing helps us reduce negative emotions, increase positive emotions, and enhance our emotional well-being.

Progressive Muscle Relaxation

Progressive muscle relaxation is a technique used to reduce stress and anxiety and manage emotional responses effectively. It involves tensing and relaxing each muscle group in your body, starting from your toes and working your way up to your head.

Here's how to do it:

1. Find a comfortable place to sit or lie down.
2. Start by focusing on your toes. Tense them for a count of five, and then relax.
3. Move up to your feet and repeat the process of tensing and relaxing.
4. Continue with your legs, stomach, hands, arms, shoulders, neck, and finally, your face.

Progressive muscle relaxation can help you become more aware of physical sensations in your body, reduce muscle tension, control stress, and manage your emotional responses more effectively.

These tools—deep breathing exercises, cognitive reframing techniques, and progressive muscle relaxation—can serve as anchors in the turbulent sea of emotions. They provide a means to keep our emotional ship steady, enabling us to navigate the waves of our feelings with greater ease and confidence. Incorporating these tools into our daily routine can enhance our ability to regulate emotions, fostering emotional balance and well-being.

As we continue our exploration of emotional regulation, we will build on the insights gained from these tools and techniques. We will learn to overcome emotional overwhelm, prioritize self-care, seek professional help, and build a support network. With each step, we move closer to achieving emotional balance, enhancing our emotional intelligence, and paving the way for a more balanced, fulfilling life.

4.3 OVERCOMING EMOTIONAL OVERWHELM: STEPS TO FREEDOM

Prioritizing Self-Care Activities

In the bustling rhythm of life, we often find ourselves juggling multiple roles and responsibilities. Amidst this whirlwind of tasks and commitments, it's easy to lose sight of a crucial aspect—self-care. Attending to your emotional well-being is not a luxury but necessary for effective emotional regulation.

So, what does self-care look like? It's as individual as we are. For some, it could be a quiet walk in the park, curling up with a good book, or engaging in a favorite hobby. The key to effective self-care is regularity and consistency.

Schedule regular "me" time in your daily routine when you engage in activities that replenish your emotional reserves. Whether it's a five-minute meditation session, a short workout, or a leisurely cup of tea, these activities can provide a much-needed pause, allowing you to recharge and manage your emotions better.

Seeking Professional Help

While self-care activities and personal emotional regulation strategies are vital, they may not be sufficient when emotional overwhelm becomes intense or prolonged. In such situations, seeking professional help can be an invaluable step toward achieving emotional balance.

Mental health professionals, such as psychologists, psychiatrists, or counselors, are trained to help individuals navigate their emotional landscape effectively. They can provide a safe, non-judgmental space for you to express your emotions, explore your triggers, and develop effective emotional regulation strategies.

If you're feeling persistently overwhelmed, anxious, or depressed, don't hesitate to seek professional help. Remember, seeking help is not a sign of weakness but a testament to your strength and commitment to your emotional well-being.

Building a Support Network

Human beings are innately social creatures. We thrive on connection, understanding, and mutual support. In the realm of emotional regulation, a robust support network can serve as a lifeline, helping us navigate emotional overwhelm and maintain emotional balance.

Your support network could include family members, friends, colleagues, or mentors—individuals who understand you, support you, and provide a listening ear when needed. They can provide perspectives you may not have considered, offer encouragement, or simply be there for you when you're feeling overwhelmed.

Building a support network involves reaching out to others, fostering relationships based on mutual respect and understanding, and being there for others when they need support. It's a reciprocal process that enhances your ability to regulate emotions and enriches your relationships and overall well-being.

Emotional overwhelm can often throw us off balance in the dynamic dance of life. But with these steps—prioritizing self-care activities, seeking professional help, and building a support network—we can regain our balance, skillfully manage our emotions, and move toward a state of emotional equilibrium. As we continue this exploration of emotional regulation, remember that each step you take brings you closer to understanding, managing, and effectively using your emotions to enhance your life.

4.4 SNAPSHOT: ACHIEVING BALANCE THROUGH EMOTIONAL REGULATION

In the vast tapestry of life, each individual thread tells a story. Some threads are vibrant, depicting tales of joy and success, while others are muted, representing struggles and hardships. One such thread is Mark's story, which takes us from emotional chaos to balance and highlights the transformative power of emotional regulation.

Mark's Struggle: From Emotional Chaos to Balance

Mark, a dedicated teacher and a loving father, was no stranger to stress. His days were filled with lesson plans, grading assignments, parent-teacher meetings, and caring for his two young children. Amid this whirlwind of responsibilities, Mark became increasingly overwhelmed by his emotions.

He would lose his temper over minor issues, feel anxious about routine tasks, and struggle with bouts of inexplicable sadness. His emotional chaos began affecting his work performance, relationships, and overall quality of life. He felt like he was on an emotional roller-coaster, with no control over his feelings.

The Strategy: A Comprehensive Approach to Emotional Regulation

Recognizing the need for change, Mark took charge of his emotional well-being. He started with self-awareness, making a conscious effort to understand his emotions. He began journaling, recording his feelings and thoughts each day. This practice helped him discern patterns in his emotional responses, identifying triggers that often led to emotional overwhelm.

With a clearer understanding of his emotional landscape, Mark focused on emotional regulation. He started practicing deep breathing exercises, using them to calm his mind during moments of stress or anxiety. He also learned cognitive reframing techniques, challenging and replacing his irrational thoughts with balanced, rational ones.

Mark also recognized the importance of self-care in emotional regulation. He started setting aside time each day for activities that he enjoyed, such as reading, gardening, or simply enjoying a quiet cup of coffee. These self-care activities served as a buffer against stress, helping him manage his emotional responses more effectively.

In addition to these personal strategies, Mark sought professional help. He began attending therapy sessions, where he learned new emotional regulation strategies and received support in managing his emotional challenges. He also built a strong support network comprising close friends, family members, and supportive colleagues, who provided emotional support and encouragement.

The Result: Improved Mental Health and Life Satisfaction

Over time, Mark began noticing changes. His emotional outbursts became less frequent, his anxiety levels reduced, and his bouts of sadness became more manageable. He found himself reacting less impulsively and responding more thoughtfully to stressful situations. His relationships improved, and he started enjoying his work again.

Mark's transformation did not happen overnight. It was a gradual process, filled with moments of progress and setbacks. But with each step, Mark moved closer to emotional balance, gaining control over his emotions rather than being controlled by them.

Mark's story serves as a testament to the power of emotional regulation. It shows us that we can manage our emotions effectively, no matter how overwhelming they seem. We can navigate our emotional landscape more easily and confidently through self-awareness, emotional regulation strategies, self-care, professional help, and a strong support network.

As we close this chapter, let's carry forward the insights from Mark's transformation. Remember that emotional regulation is not about suppressing our emotions but about understanding them, managing them, and using them to guide our journey toward emotional balance and well-being. With these insights in mind, let's continue our exploration of emotional intelligence, ready to uncover the next pillar—empathy.

EMPATHY: WALKING IN ANOTHER'S SHOES

Consider for a moment the last time you found solace in the comforting presence of a friend, a family member, or even a stranger during a moment of distress. Empathy is the soothing sense of being understood and feeling your emotions being shared. It's the gentle hand that wipes away a tear and the soft voice that whispers, "I understand." Empathy, the third pillar of emotional intelligence, transcends the boundaries of the self, connecting us with the emotions of others. It's not just about understanding our emotions but about stepping into another's shoes, seeing the world through their eyes, and sharing their emotional experience.

In this chapter, we will explore the profound world of empathy. We will delve into its significance, differentiation from sympathy, and impact on our relationships. We will also explore strategies to enhance empathy and discover how it can be applied in real-life scenarios. Let's begin this exploration by understanding a crucial differentiation—the difference between empathy and sympathy.

5.1 EMPATHY VERSUS SYMPATHY: A CRUCIAL DIFFERENTIATION

The terms empathy and sympathy are often used interchangeably, but in essence, they represent distinct emotional experiences. Sympathy is feeling for someone, while empathy is feeling with someone. Sympathy is observed from the sidelines, extending pity or concern, while empathy jumps into the game, sharing the emotional experience.

Understanding the Emotional Experience of Others

Empathy involves understanding the emotions of others. It's like tuning in to their emotional frequency, feeling their joy, sorrow, fear, and hope. Empathy is not about assuming what others might feel but about truly understanding their feelings from their perspective.

Consider a situation where a friend shares with you about losing their job. Sympathy might respond with, "I'm sorry for your loss. That's unfortunate." While there's nothing wrong with this response, it's an observation from the outside. On the other hand, empathy would involve sharing the emotional experience and responding with something like, "That must be really hard for you. I can imagine you're feeling quite upset and worried right now."

Responding with Compassion, Not Pity

One key differentiation between empathy and sympathy lies in the response. Sympathy often responds with pity, seeing the other person as an object of concern. Empathy, however, responds with compassion, recognizing the shared human experience.

In the example of the friend losing their job, a sympathetic response might be, "Poor you. I'm glad I'm not in your shoes." Though well-intentioned, this response can create a sense of separation between you and your friend. It views the friend as an object of pity rather than a fellow human being going through a difficult time.

An empathetic response, however, might be, "I'm really sorry to hear that you're going through this. Remember, it's okay to feel upset. I'm here for you." This response validates the friend's feelings and offers comfort and support, fostering a sense of shared human experience.

The Impact of Empathy on Relationships

Empathy plays a pivotal role in our relationships. It's the glue that binds people together, fostering mutual understanding and emotional connection. In any relationship, be it with friends, family, or colleagues, empathy can transform our interactions and deepen our connections.

Imagine disagreeing with your partner. In the heat of the moment, it's easy to get caught up in our perspective and insist on being right. But what if we chose empathy? What if we took a moment to understand our partner's feelings and viewpoints? This empathetic understanding can defuse conflicts, foster open communication, and deepen our relationship.

While sympathy and empathy are both responses to others' feelings, they involve different levels of emotional engagement. Sympathy is observed from the outside, extending pity or concern. Empathy, however, steps inside, sharing the emotional experience. By choosing empathy, we can enhance our relationships, foster emotional connections, and navigate our social world with greater understanding and compassion.

5.2 STRATEGIES TO ENHANCE EMPATHY

Active Listening Skills

Imagine an exchange where you feel heard, understood, and valued. Active listening is a powerful tool that transforms a routine conversation into a validating experience. Far from a passive act of hearing, active listening involves fully engaging with the speaker, both verbally and nonverbally, to understand their perspective. It's about focusing on the speaker, reflecting on their feelings, and responding with empathy.

To practice active listening, consider the following guidelines:

1. Maintain eye contact. Eye contact communicates your interest and attention, making the speaker feel valued.
2. Avoid distractions. Whether it's your phone, thoughts, or surroundings, minimizing distractions allows you to focus on the speaker and their message.
3. Reflect on the speaker's feelings. This involves acknowledging the speaker's emotions and expressing your understanding. Statements like "It sounds like you're feeling frustrated about this situation" can validate the speaker's feelings and show your empathetic understanding.
4. Provide non-verbal feedback. Nodding your head, maintaining an open body posture, and exhibiting facial expressions that align with the speaker's feelings can further enhance your empathetic engagement.

By practicing active listening, we can enhance our empathy, fostering deeper connections and mutual understanding in our relationships.

Imaginative Empathy Exercises

Empathy often involves stepping out of our perspective and stepping into another's. One way to practice this is through imaginative empathy exercises. This involves visualizing ourselves in another's situation and imagining their feelings, thoughts, and experiences.

Consider a colleague who is struggling with a challenging project. You might initiate an imaginative empathy exercise by visualizing yourself in their place. What challenges are you facing? How are you feeling about these challenges? What support would you need? This imaginative exercise can help you understand your colleague's experience at a deeper level, enhancing your empathetic response.

Remember, the aim of these exercises is not to assume what others are feeling but to enhance our capacity to understand their feelings. Practicing imaginative empathy can broaden our emotional perspective, fostering greater empathy and understanding.

Reading Fiction for Perspective-Taking

Immersing ourselves in the world of fiction can be more than a leisurely escape. It can serve as a powerful tool to enhance empathy. Whether it's a heart-wrenching drama, a thought-provoking mystery, or a soul-stirring romance, fiction invites us into the emotional lives of characters, fostering our empathetic understanding.

As you read, pay attention to the characters' emotions, thoughts, and experiences. How do their feelings change throughout the story? What challenges do they face, and how do they cope with them? How would you feel if you were in their place?

By reading fiction, we practice perspective-taking, stepping into the shoes of diverse characters, and understanding their emotional experiences. This practice can enhance our empathy, equipping us to understand others' feelings more effectively in real life.

These strategies—active listening, imaginative empathy exercises, and reading fiction—provide practical ways to enhance empathy. By incorporating these strategies into our routine, we can foster our empathetic understanding, leading to deeper connections, better communication, and enhanced emotional intelligence.

5.3 EMPATHY IN ACTION: REAL-LIFE SCENARIOS

Empathy in the Workplace: A Case Study

Picture a bustling corporate office. Amid the hum of activity, Tom is a project manager known for his efficiency and commitment. One day, a member of Tom's team, Sarah, starts missing deadlines, and her work quality declines. Instead of reprimanding Sarah for her performance dip, Tom approaches the situation empathetically.

Tom schedules a one-on-one meeting with Sarah, creating a safe space for open dialogue. He expresses his concern about her recent performance, not with criticism, but with understanding. He asks Sarah about any challenges she might be facing and how he can support her.

Feeling heard and valued, Sarah opens up about her struggles with balancing work and personal life due to a family crisis. Tom empathizes with her situation, and together, they develop a flexible work plan that accommodates Sarah's current circumstances.

In this scenario, empathy transformed a potential conflict into a supportive conversation. Tom's empathetic approach helped Sarah and fostered a supportive team environment, boosting overall team morale.

Empathy in Parenting: A Personal Account

Now, let's focus on a different setting—a family home. Meet Emily, a mother of two. One afternoon, Emily finds her 10-year-old son, Ben, upset over losing a football match at school. Instead of dismissing his feelings as trivial or lecturing him about the importance of sportsmanship, Emily responds with empathy.

She sits down with Ben, acknowledges his disappointment, and validates his feelings. Emily shares a story from her childhood about a time she felt similarly after losing a school competition. She reassures Ben that it's okay to feel upset and that these feelings will pass.

At this moment, Emily's empathy helps Ben feel understood and comforted. Her empathetic response also taught Ben a crucial life lesson about acknowledging and managing emotions.

Empathy in Friendship: An Anecdote

Our final stop in exploring empathy in action is a college campus. Here, we find Alex and Sam, best friends and roommates. One day, Sam receives a lower-than-expected grade on a crucial exam. He feels disappointed and worried about his academic standing.

Instead of offering advice or trying to cheer Sam up, Alex responds with empathy. He acknowledges Sam's disappointment and concerns about the academic implications. Alex reflects on Sam's feelings, saying, "It sounds like you're really disappointed with your grade and worried about what this could mean for your GPA."

In this instance, Alex's empathy reinforced the bond of their friendship. His empathetic response showed Sam that his feelings were understood and shared, offering him comfort in his moment of stress.

These real-life scenarios illustrate the power of empathy in action. From the bustling corporate office to the family home, from the college campus to the countless settings we encounter, empathy can transform our interactions and deepen our connections. It reminds us that there's a shared human experience and emotional landscape at the heart of every interaction. And it is empathy that allows us to navigate this landscape with understanding, compassion, and genuine connection.

5.4 PERSONAL STORY: A JOURNEY TOWARD EMPATHY

Lisa's Story: From Emotional Isolation to Connection

Meet Lisa, a dedicated software developer known for her technical prowess and innovative solutions. However, when it came to social interactions, Lisa often found herself lost. She struggled to understand others' feelings and often felt disconnected during conversations. She tried to fit in and connect, but her attempts were like trying to tune a radio to a frequency that she couldn't quite catch. This emotional isolation often left her feeling lonely and misunderstood.

The Catalyst: An Unexpected Friendship

Life, however, had a surprising turn in store for Lisa. At a team-building workshop, Lisa was paired with Mia, a colleague from the HR department. Mia was known for her people skills, ability to connect with others, and empathy. As they worked together on various tasks, Lisa was drawn to Mia's warm and understanding nature. She felt heard and valued in a way she hadn't experienced before.

This connection sparked a curiosity in Lisa. She started wondering about empathy and its role in relationships. Intrigued, she delved into books, articles, and online courses, eager to learn about empathy. She discovered the world of emotional intelligence and realized that what she had been struggling with was a lack of empathy.

The Transformation: Enhanced Relationships and Personal Growth

Armed with her newfound knowledge, Lisa decided to cultivate empathy. She started practicing active listening, paying full attention to others during conversations. She began to express her feelings more openly and encouraged others to do the same. She consciously tried to understand others' perspectives, even when they differed from hers.

The change was gradual but tangible. Lisa noticed a shift in her interactions. Conversations that she previously found daunting became opportunities for connection. She started understanding her colleagues better, fostering stronger relationships. Her emotional isolation started giving way to a sense of belonging.

Lisa's transformation didn't stop in her professional life. She noticed changes in her personal relationships as well. She became more understanding and patient with her family members, strengthening their bonds. She formed deeper connections with her friends, enhancing her social life.

Lisa's journey from emotional isolation to connection underscores the transformative power of empathy. It reminds us that empathy is not an inborn trait but a skill that can be learned and cultivated. It shows that embracing empathy can enhance our relationships, foster connection, and enrich our emotional lives.

Lisa's transformation brought her a newfound sense of belonging in her personal and professional life. Her story stands as an example of the transformative power of empathy, inspiring us to cultivate this essential emotional skill.

As we conclude this chapter, we carry forward the understanding of empathy as an integral part of emotional intelligence. It's a skill that enables us to connect with others on a deeper level, fostering mutual understanding and emotional connection. As we move forward, we'll continue to explore the fascinating landscape of emotional intelligence, ready to uncover the next pillar—emotional agility.

MAKE A DIFFERENCE WITH YOUR REVIEW

UNLOCK THE POWER OF GENEROSITY

"Kindness is a language which the deaf can hear and the blind can see."

— MARK TWAIN

Helping others gives us a sense of joy unlike any other. Imagine the happiness you can bring to someone's life with just a few kind words. That's the magic we believe in at MindfulMinds Co.

Would you be willing to share a little kindness with someone seeking guidance in emotional intelligence? Someone just like you, who is on the path to understanding their emotions and improving their relationships.

Our goal at MindfulMinds Co. is to make the wisdom of emotional intelligence accessible to everyone. To spread this knowledge far and wide, we need your help.

Your review can light the way for others to find the tools they need for personal growth. It's a simple act that takes less than a minute but can profoundly impact someone's life. Here's how you can contribute:

- Leave a review and share your experience with the book.
- Use this link https://www.amazon.com/review/create-review/?asin=B0D2L474D7 or scan the QR code below

By helping others discover this book, you become a part of their journey toward emotional intelligence. Welcome to a community of kindness and growth.

Thank you deeply for your support and for being a beacon of positive change.

Your friends at MindfulMinds Co.

P.S. Sharing valuable insights makes you invaluable to others. If this book has touched your life, consider passing it on to someone who could also benefit from it.

EMOTIONAL INTELLIGENCE: THE INTERSECTION WITH MINDFULNESS

Every breath we take is an invitation and opportunity to pause, to anchor ourselves in the present moment. In this moment, away from the tumult of the past and the uncertainty of the future, we find mindfulness. This practice, rooted in ancient wisdom and validated by modern science, is a pathway to enhanced emotional intelligence. It highlights the intricate dance between our breath, mind, and emotions, highlighting their deep interconnection and mutual influence.

In this chapter, we will explore mindfulness, its benefits, and its connection with emotional intelligence. We will navigate this uncharted territory with curiosity, openness, and a keen desire to understand mindfulness's profound impact on our emotional landscape.

6.1 UNDERSTANDING MINDFULNESS: A BASIC GUIDE

Definition of Mindfulness

At its core, mindfulness is about being fully present in the moment. It's about engaging with the here and now, observing our thoughts, feelings, and sensations without judgment. It's like sitting by a river, watching the water flow—noticing the ripples, currents, ebb, and flow but not trying to change or control it.

Imagine you're sipping a cup of coffee. Mindfulness is about fully engaging with this experience. It's about feeling the warmth of the cup in your hand, smelling the rich aroma of the coffee, and tasting its unique flavor on your tongue. It's not about planning your day or worrying about your to-do list. It's about being fully present with your cup of coffee.

Benefits of Mindfulness

The practice of mindfulness offers a plethora of benefits. Let's consider a few:

- Reduced Stress: Mindfulness helps us step back from the whirlwind of thoughts and worries that often fuel stress. It encourages us to focus on the present moment, reducing anxiety and promoting relaxation.
- Enhanced Focus: Mindfulness can improve our attention span and concentration by training our minds to focus on the present. Whether it's a complex task at work or a conversation with a friend, mindfulness enables us to engage fully, enhancing our performance and the quality of our interactions.

- Improved Emotional Well-Being: Mindfulness helps us observe our emotions without getting swept up in them. We learn to experience our feelings without judgment or resistance, promoting emotional balance and well-being.
- Increased Self-Awareness: Mindfulness sharpens our internal lens, enabling us to observe our thoughts, feelings, and sensations more clearly. This enhanced self-awareness is a key component of emotional intelligence.

Mindfulness and Emotional Intelligence: The Connection

Mindfulness and emotional intelligence are two sides of the same coin. They intersect and interact in profound ways, each enriching and supporting the other.

Consider the core components of emotional intelligence: self-awareness, emotional regulation, and empathy. Each is deeply rooted in mindfulness.

- Self-Awareness and Mindfulness: Mindfulness enhances self-awareness. Practicing mindfulness teaches us to observe our thoughts and emotions without judgment. We become more attuned to our internal state, improving our self-awareness.
- Emotional Regulation and Mindfulness: Mindfulness promotes emotional regulation. By observing our emotions non-judgmentally, we can recognize when they are intensifying and use mindfulness techniques to manage our emotional responses.
- Empathy and Mindfulness: Mindfulness fosters empathy. As we become more mindful of our emotions, we can better understand and share the emotions of others.

In essence, mindfulness is not just a complementary practice to emotional intelligence; it's an integral part of it. By cultivating mindfulness, we enhance our emotional intelligence, equipping ourselves with the skills to navigate the emotional landscape of our lives with greater ease and effectiveness.

As we continue to explore mindfulness and its intersection with emotional intelligence, remember that this practice, like any other skill, requires patience and consistency. It's not about attaining a state of constant calm or emptying our minds of thoughts. It's about cultivating an attitude of openness and curiosity toward our present-moment experience, be it pleasant or unpleasant, exciting or mundane. It's about learning to be with what is, fully and wholeheartedly.

6.2 MINDFULNESS TECHNIQUES FOR ENHANCED EMOTIONAL INTELLIGENCE

The world of mindfulness offers a plethora of practices designed to anchor us in the present moment, heighten our awareness, and enrich our understanding of ourselves. These practices include mindful breathing, body scan meditation, and mindful observation. Each technique offers a unique pathway to enhance emotional intelligence, enabling us to navigate our emotional landscape with greater ease and efficacy.

Mindful Breathing

Breathing is a natural and essential part of our lives. We do it without thinking, every moment of every day. But when we bring our full attention to it, this simple act transforms into a powerful tool for mindfulness. Mindful breathing is observing the breath as it flows in and out without trying to change or control it. It's about noticing how the breath feels, where we feel it most prominently, and how it changes from moment to moment.

To practice mindful breathing, find a comfortable place to sit or lie down. Close your eyes and bring your attention to your breath. Notice how the air feels as it enters your nostrils, fills your lungs, and then leaves your body. Observe the rhythm of your breath, the rise and fall of your chest or abdomen. If your mind wanders, gently bring it back to your breath.

Mindful breathing serves as an anchor, grounding us in the present moment. It enhances self-awareness, helping us notice subtle changes in our emotional state. For instance, you might observe that your breath becomes shallow and quick when you're anxious or deep and slow when you're relaxed. This awareness can provide valuable insights into your emotions, enhancing your emotional intelligence.

Body Scan Meditation

Body scan meditation is another effective mindfulness technique. It involves mentally scanning your body from head to toe and observing any sensations, tensions, or emotions that arise. It's like taking a "tour" of your body, visiting each part with curiosity and openness.

To practice body scan meditation, start by finding a comfortable position. Close your eyes and take a few deep breaths to center yourself. Then, start scanning your body from your toes, moving upwards through your legs, abdomen, chest, arms, and finally, to your head. As you scan each part of your body, observe any sensations you feel. It could be tension, relaxation, warmth, coolness, or even numbness.

Body scan meditation helps us to connect with our physical selves, fostering a sense of embodied awareness. It enables us to notice the interplay between our bodies and our emotions. For instance, you might notice that your shoulders tense up when you're stressed or that your heart rate increases when you're excited. This awareness of bodily sensations associated with different emotions can enhance your emotional intelligence, aiding in recognizing and understanding your feelings.

Mindful Observation

Mindful observation involves fully engaging with our surroundings, observing them with curiosity and without judgment. It's about truly seeing rather than merely looking.

To practice mindful observation, choose an object in your surroundings. It could be a plant, a cloud, a coffee mug, or even your own hand. Observe this object as if you're seeing it for the first time. Notice its colors, textures, and shape. If it's a living thing, observe how it moves. If it's stationary, observe its stillness.

Mindful observation helps us step out of our inner world of thoughts and emotions, grounding us in the external world. It provides a break from our emotional chatter, offering a moment of calm and clarity. Moreover, it enhances our ability to observe emotions in ourselves and others, an essential aspect of emotional intelligence.

These mindfulness techniques—mindful breathing, body scan meditation, and mindful observation—offer practical ways to enhance our emotional intelligence. By incorporating these practices into our daily routine, we can cultivate a mindset of mindfulness, fostering self-awareness, emotional regulation, and empathy. The key to these practices is consistency and patience. So, as you breathe, scan, and observe, remember to do so with kindness toward yourself, knowing that you're cultivating a deeper connection with your emotional self with each mindful moment.

6.3 HOW MINDFULNESS IMPROVES EMOTIONAL RESPONSE

Enhanced Self-Awareness

The practice of mindfulness cultivates a heightened state of self-awareness. It is akin to turning up the volume on a radio, allowing the subtle notes of the music, previously unheard, to reach our ears. Similarly, mindfulness amplifies our inner emotional symphony, enabling us to hear and understand each note, rhythm, and pause.

An integral aspect of mindfulness is focused attention, which we direct toward our emotions. As we sit in silence, we tune into our emotional state, observing the ebb and flow of our feelings. We notice our joy, sorrow, fear, and calm, not as distant observers but as active participants in our emotional experience.

This focused attention on our emotions allows us to recognize our feelings, understand their nature, and discern their triggers. We see the connection between an external event and our emotional response, discerning patterns and associations. Understanding our emotional landscape is the bedrock of self-awareness, a crucial component of emotional intelligence.

Improved Emotional Regulation

Mindfulness and emotional regulation are closely intertwined, each reinforcing the other in a positive feedback loop. As we cultivate mindfulness, we can effectively regulate our emotional responses. On the other hand, as our ability to regulate emotions improves, it enhances our mindfulness practice, leading to a deeper, richer experience.

Imagine watching a storm from the safety of your home. You see the lightning, hear the thunder, and feel the vibrations, but the storm does not sweep you away. You're observing and experiencing it, but you're not a part of it. Mindfulness offers a similar experience with our emotions. We observe our feelings, experience them fully, but don't get swept away by them.

This ability to observe our emotions without getting overwhelmed by them is the essence of emotional regulation. It allows us to experience our feelings and validate them but not let them dictate our thoughts or actions. We can choose how we respond to our emotions by taking a deep breath, practicing a mindfulness exercise, or seeking support.

Increased Empathy

Empathy, the ability to understand and share the feelings of others, is a natural outcome of regular mindfulness practice. As we become more attuned to our emotions, we develop the capacity to tune into the emotional experiences of others. It's like learning a new language. Once we're fluent in the language of our own emotions, we can understand the emotional language of others.

Picture yourself sitting across from a friend who's sharing a distressing experience. As they speak, you observe their body language, tone of voice, and choice of words. You notice the subtle changes in their expressions, silent pauses, and unshed tears. Your mindfulness practice allows you to tune into these subtle cues, enhancing your empathic understanding.

This ability to empathize, to understand and share the feelings of others, can transform our relationships. It fosters a deep connection, mutual understanding, and emotional support. Whether with family, friends, colleagues, or even strangers, empathy can enhance our interactions and enrich our social and emotional lives.

We can enhance our emotional intelligence through mindfulness, cultivating self-awareness, emotional regulation, and empathy. This does not require a drastic lifestyle change or hours of meditation. It's about incorporating small moments of mindfulness into our daily lives, moments where we pause, breathe, and connect with our inner emotional world. With each mindful moment, we step closer to understanding, managing, and effectively using our emotions to enhance our lives.

6.4 EXPERIENCE REPORT: EMOTIONAL GROWTH THROUGH MINDFULNESS

Personal Story of Emotional Transformation

Let's turn our gaze toward the life of Anna, a dedicated healthcare professional. Known for her technical expertise and commitment to her patients, Anna was always on the go. Her days were a whirlwind of medical procedures, patient consultations, and paperwork. Amidst this frenzy of activities, she often felt overwhelmed and emotionally drained. She longed for a sense of calm, a moment of silence, and a chance to reconnect with herself.

This longing led Anna to the practice of mindfulness. Intrigued by its promise of inner peace and emotional balance, she decided to try it. She started with a simple practice of mindful breathing, taking a few minutes each day to focus on her breath. She also started incorporating mindfulness into her daily activities, whether savoring her morning cup of coffee or walking mindfully from her car to the hospital.

Challenges Faced and Overcome

The path to mindfulness, however, was not always smooth. Like many of us, Anna struggled with distractions, impatience, and self-doubt. There were days when she felt too busy to practice mindfulness, days when her mind seemed uncontrollably chaotic, and days when she questioned the effectiveness of her practice.

But Anna didn't give up. She reminded herself that mindfulness is not about achieving a perfect state of calm or mastering control over her thoughts. Instead, it's about observing her experiences, thoughts, and emotions without judgment. With this understanding, she persisted in her practice, embracing the chaos, the calm, and everything in between.

Lessons Learned and Insights Gained

Over time, Anna noticed changes. She felt less overwhelmed by her emotions and more connected to her inner self. She started recognizing her emotional triggers, understanding their influence on her thoughts and behaviors, and managing them more effectively. She found herself responding to stressful situations with a sense of calm and clarity instead of reacting impulsively.

Anna's transformation did not stop in her personal life. She noticed changes in her professional interactions as well. She became more patient with her patients, understanding their fears and concerns with a newfound empathy. She dealt with workplace challenges with resilience and grace, leading to improved performance and job satisfaction.

Anna's experience serves as a testament to the transformative power of mindfulness. It shows us that mindfulness is not an elusive concept confined to meditation cushions or yoga studios. It's a practical, accessible tool that we can incorporate into our daily lives, a tool that can lead us toward enhanced emotional intelligence.

As Anna's story illustrates, the path to mindfulness might not always be smooth, and the transformation might not be instant. But with patience, consistency, and curiosity, we can cultivate mindfulness, enhancing our self-awareness, emotional regulation, and empathy. With each mindful breath and moment, we step closer to a greater understanding of ourselves and our emotions, paving the way for a more balanced, fulfilling life.

With the insights gleaned from exploring mindfulness and its intersection with emotional intelligence, we are now ready to delve deeper into emotional intelligence. In the following chapters, we will explore further aspects of emotional intelligence, including emotional resilience and emotional agility, equipping ourselves with a comprehensive understanding of this powerful concept.

BUILDING RESILIENCE: THE EMOTIONAL SHIELD

In the grand theatre of life, we are both an actor and a spectator. We participate in the drama, laugh at the comedy, and occasionally shed tears in the tragedy. But what happens when the curtain falls on a scene of adversity, a tableau of hardship and despair? In these moments, we glance at the script of resilience, which empowers us to face adversity, endure hardships, and emerge stronger. Resilience, an integral component of emotional intelligence, is the emotional shield that guards us against life's challenges and helps us bounce back with renewed vigor.

To understand resilience, let's first take a moment to define it.

7.1 THE CONCEPT OF RESILIENCE: AN OVERVIEW

Definition of Resilience

Resilience is the psychological strength that enables us to cope with stress and adversity. It's not about avoiding difficulties but about facing them with courage, learning from the experiences, and moving forward. Picture resilience as a rubber band. When stretched by adverse circumstances, it expands. But once the stress is removed, it bounces back to its original shape, sometimes even stretching a little further than before, symbolizing growth from the experience.

Importance of Resilience in Emotional Intelligence

Resilience and emotional intelligence are intricately linked. Emotional intelligence provides the tools for resilience. It involves recognizing our emotions (self-awareness), managing them effectively (self-regulation), and understanding others' emotions (empathy). These tools equip us to face life's challenges, adapt to change, and bounce back from adversity—the essence of resilience.

Consider a scenario where you're faced with a significant setback at work—maybe you've been passed over for a promotion, or a project you've been working on has failed. Emotional intelligence would guide you to recognize and accept your disappointment (self-awareness), manage your emotional response effectively (self-regulation), and consider the perspectives and feelings of others involved (empathy). These emotionally intelligent responses pave the way for resilience, enabling you to learn from the experience and move forward.

Benefits of Resilience

The benefits of resilience extend beyond coping with stress and adversity. It's like a multi-purpose tool, offering a range of benefits that enhance our personal and professional lives. Here are a few:

- Improved Mental Health: Resilience helps us manage

stress and reduces the risk of mental health issues such as anxiety and depression.
- Enhanced Performance: Resilience enables us to maintain our performance in the face of challenges or setbacks, learn from the experience, and apply what we have learned in the future.
- Better Relationships: Resilience equips us to handle conflicts and challenges in our relationships, fostering understanding, harmony, and mutual respect.
- Greater Life Satisfaction: By helping us cope with life's ups and downs, resilience contributes to a sense of contentment and overall life satisfaction.

The concept of resilience, with its definition, importance, and benefits, presents a compelling narrative about the human spirit's capacity to endure, adapt, and grow. It's a narrative of hope, courage, and an unwavering belief in our ability to navigate life's challenges. As we journey further into emotional intelligence, let's carry forward this narrative, ready to explore strategies that foster emotional resilience, understand its role in facing adversity, and celebrate its triumphs.

7.2 TECHNIQUES TO FOSTER EMOTIONAL RESILIENCE

Resilience is akin to a muscle that grows stronger with consistent practice and the proper training regimen. Let's explore three powerful exercises to enhance our emotional resilience—positive affirmations, cognitive reframing, and building a support network.

Positive Affirmations

A Window to a Positive Mindset

Have you ever noticed how your thoughts can shape your mood, day, and actions? Positive affirmations are a tool to harness this power of thought, steering your mind toward positivity and resilience. They are concise, powerful statements that promote a positive mindset, reinforce self-belief, and boost self-esteem.

Crafting and Practicing Positive Affirmations

To create your positive affirmations, focus on your strengths, values, and goals. Frame your affirmations in the present tense, make them positive, and keep them brief. For instance, instead of saying, "I will not let stress control me," say, "I am calm and in control, even in stressful situations."

Practice your affirmations daily, preferably at the same time each day—it could be as soon as you wake up, during a midday break, or before going to bed. As you repeat your affirmations, visualize them, believe in them, and you'll start to notice a shift toward a more positive and resilient mindset.

Cognitive Reframing

A Lens of Perspective

Imagine looking at a picture through different colored lenses. Each lens brings out a unique aspect of the picture, offering a new perspective. Cognitive reframing works similarly. It involves shifting our perspective of a situation, changing a negative viewpoint into a positive one, thereby promoting resilience.

Implementing Cognitive Reframing

To practice cognitive reframing, start by observing your thoughts, particularly in challenging situations. Identify any negative or irrational thoughts and challenge their validity. Then, try to find a positive or rational alternative.

For instance, if you catch yourself thinking, "I always mess up," challenge this thought: Is it really always? Then, reframe it by finding a positive or balanced alternative: "I may have made a mistake this time, but I've also had many successes. I can learn from this experience and improve."

Cognitive reframing fosters resilience and enhances emotional intelligence by promoting self-awareness and effective emotional regulation.

Building a Support Network

A Circle of Empathy and Understanding

Life's challenges become a little less daunting when faced with the support and understanding of others. A robust support network provides emotional support, practical help, and a sense of belonging, fostering resilience.

Nurturing Your Support Network

Your support network could include family, friends, colleagues, mentors, or even support groups. Foster these relationships with open communication, empathy, and mutual respect. Be there for them in their times of need, and don't hesitate to reach out when you need support.

A strong support network provides a safety net during challenging times and enriches our lives with meaningful relationships and shared experiences. It fosters resilience by reminding us that we are not alone in our struggles and have the strength and support to bounce back from adversity.

These techniques—positive affirmations, cognitive reframing, and building a support network—offer practical ways to enhance emotional resilience. By incorporating these techniques into our routine, we can strengthen our emotional resilience, equipping ourselves to face life's challenges with courage, learn from our experiences, and bounce back stronger. Each step toward fostering resilience brings us closer to a state of emotional balance, equipping us to navigate the ebb and flow of life's challenges with grace and fortitude.

7.3 RESILIENCE IN THE FACE OF ADVERSITY: HOW TO BOUNCE BACK

Life, with its ups and downs, joys and sorrows, victories and defeats, is rife with adversities. No matter how unwelcome, these challenging episodes can serve as catalysts for personal growth if navigated with resilience. Bouncing back from adversity is not about avoiding hardships but acknowledging them, understanding the emotions they evoke, and utilizing the experience for personal development. This process involves three critical steps: recognizing and accepting emotions, learning from mistakes and failures, and cultivating a growth mindset.

Recognizing and Accepting Emotions

When we encounter adversity, our first instinct might be to suppress the negative emotions that arise. We may try to put on a brave face, convincing ourselves and others that "everything is fine." However, this avoidance can lead to emotional bottlenecks, hindering our path to resilience. The first step toward resilience is recognizing and accepting our emotions.

When adversity hits, take a moment to connect with your feelings. Are you feeling disappointed, scared, frustrated, or sad? Acknowledge these emotions. Give yourself permission to feel them. Remember, it's okay to feel upset when faced with challenges. Accepting your emotions doesn't mean dwelling on them. Instead, it's about understanding that it's normal for humans to experience such feelings. This recognition and acceptance create a solid foundation for emotional resilience, preparing us to navigate the next phase: learning from our mistakes and failures.

Learning from Mistakes and Failures

Mistakes and failures are often seen as the villains in our life story. We view them as stumbling blocks, signs of inadequacy, or reasons for embarrassment. But what if we could change the narrative? What if we could view mistakes and failures as stepping stones to success, as opportunities for learning and growth?

When faced with adversity, take a step back and reflect on the situation. Were there mistakes made? What led to these mistakes? How can these mistakes be avoided in the future? This introspective examination transforms mistakes and failures from hurdles to stepping stones on the path to success.

Similarly, failures can serve as powerful teachers. Instead of viewing a failed attempt as a dead end, consider it a detour—an opportunity to learn, adapt, and grow. Each failure brings you one step closer to success, equipping you with valuable insights and experiences. This shift in perspective, from viewing mistakes and failures as threats to seeing them as opportunities, paves the way for the final step toward resilience: developing a growth mindset.

Developing a Growth Mindset

The concept of mindset refers to our beliefs about abilities and potential. A growth mindset, a term coined by psychologist Carol Dweck, is the belief that our abilities can be developed through dedication and hard work. It's about viewing challenges as opportunities for growth, effort as a pathway to mastery, and criticism as a source of learning.

When we cultivate a growth mindset, we view adversity from a different lens. We see it not as a confirmation of our limitations but as an opportunity to grow beyond our current abilities. A setback is no longer a roadblock but a sign that we need to employ new strategies or put in more effort. Criticism transforms from a source of discouragement to a wellspring of constructive feedback.

Cultivating a growth mindset involves recognizing our growth potential, embracing challenges, persisting in the face of setbacks, viewing effort as a path to mastery, and learning from criticism. As we foster this mindset, we equip ourselves with a potent tool for resilience, enabling us to bounce back from adversity with renewed determination and an unwavering belief in our ability to grow.

Bouncing back from adversity is a testament to the human spirit's resilience. It's about recognizing and accepting our emotions, learning from our mistakes and failures, and fostering a growth mindset. Each step brings us closer to resilience, equipping us to face life's adversities not with fear or avoidance but with courage, understanding, and an unwavering belief in our ability to bounce back.

7.4 RESILIENCE TRIUMPH: A REAL-LIFE ACCOUNT

Think of the human spirit as a resilient tree. Even in the harshest of winters, it stands tall, enduring the biting cold and the weight of the snow. And when spring arrives, it blossoms, bearing signs of growth and renewal. Our story of resilience echoes this spirit of endurance and growth—the story of John and his transformation from a phase of adversity to a state of accomplishment.

Personal Story of Overcoming Adversity

John, an accomplished entrepreneur, had always prided himself on his business acumen and strong work ethic. His venture was thriving, and success seemed to be his constant companion. Until one day, it wasn't. A sudden economic downturn hit his business hard. He faced mounting debts, dwindling revenues, and the looming threat of bankruptcy.

In the face of this daunting adversity, John grappled with intense emotions. There was fear about the future of his venture, anxiety about financial stability, and a deep sense of disappointment. It felt like he was adrift in a turbulent sea of adversity with no shore in sight.

Role of Resilience in Success

However, instead of surrendering to the storm, John chose to navigate it. He realized that overcoming this adversity was not by avoiding or suppressing his emotions but by acknowledging and managing them. He began to recognize his feelings of fear, anxiety, and disappointment. He allowed himself to feel these emotions, understanding they were natural responses to his situation.

John also started to view his situation from a different perspective. Instead of seeing it as a failure, he saw it as a challenge, an opportunity to learn and grow. He began to reframe his thoughts, replacing negative assumptions with positive affirmations. Instead of thinking, "I've failed, and I can't recover from this," he would tell himself, "This is a tough phase, but I have the strength and the skills to overcome it."

In addition to managing his emotions and thoughts, John reached out to others. He connected with fellow entrepreneurs, sharing his experiences and learning from theirs. He sought guidance from mentors, gaining new insights and strategies. He leaned on his family and friends for emotional support, drawing strength from their faith in him.

Key Takeaways and Lessons Learned

As John navigated his way through adversity, he noticed a shift. His fear began to recede, replaced by a sense of determination. His anxiety gave way to confidence. His disappointment transformed into motivation. He was no longer adrift in the sea of adversity; he was sailing through it, charting his course with resilience.

John's business gradually started to recover. He implemented new strategies, learned from past mistakes, and adapted to the changing economic landscape. His venture, once on the brink of bankruptcy, was now thriving again. But the real triumph was not just his business's recovery but the transformation of his spirit.

John's story is a testament to the power of resilience. It shows us that adversity can be overcome with emotional intelligence and resilience, no matter how daunting. It reminds us that emotions when recognized and managed effectively, can be our allies in the face of challenges. It highlights the importance of a positive mindset, a supportive network, and an unwavering belief in our ability to bounce back.

As we close this chapter, let's carry forward the spirit of resilience. Remember that every adversity we encounter is an opportunity for growth, every challenge a stepping stone to success, and every setback a setup for a comeback. As we step into the next chapter, let's prepare to explore another fascinating aspect of emotional intelligence—emotional agility, with the strength of resilience echoing in our steps.

EMOTIONAL AGILITY: DANCE WITH YOUR EMOTIONS

Picture yourself on a dance floor. The music changes rhythm unpredictably, switching from a slow waltz to a fast-paced tango and then to a lively salsa. As a dancer, your success lies not in resisting these changes but in adapting to them, moving fluidly with the shifting rhythms. Emotional agility is much like this dance. It's about flexibly adapting to our ever-changing emotions, not getting stuck in rigid patterns, and being able to move with the ebb and flow of our emotional currents.

8.1 EMOTIONAL AGILITY DEFINED: THE NEW AGE CONCEPT

Definition of Emotional Agility

Emotional agility is a relatively new concept in the field of emotional intelligence, introduced by psychologist Susan David. It refers to the ability to navigate our inner world of thoughts and emotions with flexibility, adapting to the shifting patterns without getting stuck in rigid responses. It's about recognizing our emotions, understanding what they're telling us, and then choosing a response that aligns with our values and serves our overall well-being.

Think of emotional agility as a bridge between your emotions and your actions. On one end of the bridge, you have your emotions—complex, often intense, and constantly changing. On the other end, you have your actions—the choices you make and the steps you take in response to your emotions. The bridge of emotional agility ensures that your actions align with your emotions in a constructive, adaptive, and values-aligned way.

Importance of Emotional Agility in Emotional Intelligence

Emotional agility plays a crucial role in emotional intelligence. It's the dynamic, flexible aspect of emotional intelligence, complementing the more static components—self-awareness, emotional regulation, and empathy. While these components provide a solid foundation for understanding and managing our emotions, emotional agility adds the element of adaptability, enhancing our capacity to navigate the fluid landscape of our emotions.

Imagine viewing your emotions through a kaleidoscope. Each twist presents a new pattern, a different combination of colors and shapes. Emotional agility is the ability to adapt to each twist and new pattern without losing sight of the overall picture.

Benefits of Emotional Agility

The practice of emotional agility offers many benefits. It equips us with the skills to effectively handle emotional transitions, enhances our decision-making abilities, and contributes to our overall emotional well-being.

- Handling Emotional Transitions: Life is full of emotional transitions. Whether it's a career change, a relationship shift, or a personal loss, these transitions often bring a wave of different emotions. Emotional agility allows us to navigate these transitions gracefully, adapting to the changing emotions and managing our responses effectively.
- Enhanced Decision-Making: Our emotions can significantly influence our decisions. Emotional agility helps us to understand these influences, ensuring intense emotions do not impulsively drive our decisions. It ensures our decisions are balanced and aligned with our values.
- Improved Emotional Well-Being: By promoting a flexible and adaptive approach to managing emotions, emotional agility contributes to our emotional well-being. It helps us to maintain emotional balance, even in the face of adversity, fostering resilience and enhancing our overall quality of life.

The concept of emotional agility, with its emphasis on flexibility, adaptability, and values-aligned actions, paints a dynamic picture of emotional intelligence. It's a dance with our emotions, a dance that is not choreographed to a fixed rhythm but one that adapts and flows with the changing music of our emotional landscape. As we delve deeper into emotional intelligence, let's keep this picture in mind and get ready to explore more facets of this intriguing dance.

8.2 STRATEGIES FOR DEVELOPING EMOTIONAL AGILITY

Emotional agility, a nuanced and dynamic component of emotional intelligence, requires a balanced, receptive, and active approach. It is about acknowledging our emotions, detaching from unhelpful thoughts, and taking values-based actions. Like navigating a river with a current that changes its course, these strategies offer a pathway to emotional balance and well-being.

Accepting and Labeling Emotions

The first step toward emotional agility is embracing our emotions with an accepting attitude. Acceptance does not mean resignation or passive submission. Rather, it is about acknowledging our emotions without judgment, recognizing they are a natural response to our experiences.

For instance, if you feel a surge of anxiety before a big presentation, acknowledge this feeling. Instead of trying to push it away or ignoring it, simply observe it. Recognize that it's natural to feel anxious in such situations.

Labeling our emotions is an effective way to acknowledge them. Assigning a name to what we are feeling can provide a sense of control and help reduce the intensity of the emotion. For example, instead of thinking, "I'm feeling bad," you could say to yourself, "I'm feeling anxious because I have a presentation." This specificity can provide clarity and create some emotional distance, preventing you from becoming engulfed by the emotion.

Detaching from Unhelpful Thoughts

Just as a mirror reflects an image without holding onto it, our minds can learn to observe thoughts without clinging to them. We often get entangled in our thoughts, especially negative or distressing ones. Detachment involves observing our thoughts as temporary, passing events rather than definitive truths.

Suppose you find yourself caught in a whirlwind of self-critical thoughts after making a mistake. Instead of identifying with these thoughts, you can choose to observe them as an impartial witness. You might say to yourself, "I'm having the thought that I am not good enough," instead of, "I am not good enough." This subtle shift in perspective can help to detach from unhelpful thoughts, reducing their impact on your emotions and actions.

Taking Values-Based Actions

While accepting and labeling emotions and detaching from unhelpful thoughts are receptive strategies, taking values-based actions is an active strategy. This involves making choices and taking actions that align with our values, even in the face of challenging emotions.

Imagine you have a difficult conversation that you have been avoiding due to fear of conflict. However, one of your core values is honesty in your relationships. In this situation, a values-based action would be to have the conversation, despite the fear, because it aligns with your value of honesty.

Taking values-based actions requires clarity about our core values. Reflecting on what truly matters to us can provide this clarity. Whether it's integrity, compassion, growth, or authenticity, having a clear understanding of our values can guide our actions, helping us to live authentically and enhance our emotional well-being.

Cultivating emotional agility is like learning a new dance. It requires practice, patience, and perseverance. But with each step, each twirl, and each leap, we become more adept at navigating the changing rhythms of our emotions. We learn to flow with the music of life, embracing its highs and lows with grace, courage, and resilience. The dance of emotional agility is a dance of life itself, a dance that celebrates our emotional complexity and our capacity for growth and transformation. So, let's keep dancing, growing, and exploring the fascinating landscape of emotional intelligence.

8.3 EMOTIONAL AGILITY AT WORK: A PRACTICAL SCENARIO

In the bustling corridors of the corporate world, emotional agility can be a game-changer. Whether managing stress, navigating office politics, or achieving work-life balance, emotional agility equips us with the skills to face these challenges effectively. Let's explore how we can apply emotional agility in these three common work situations.

Dealing with Workplace Stress

Workplace stress is like a persistent shadow, often lurking around tight deadlines, high expectations, and challenging tasks. In the face of this stress, emotional agility encourages us to pause and tune into our emotions.

Suppose you're grappling with a demanding project with a rapidly approaching deadline. The stress levels are escalating, and you feel a surge of anxiety. Instead of getting swept away by this anxiety, you can choose to acknowledge it. You can observe the anxiety without judgment, understanding that it's a natural response to the situation.

Next, you can detach from any unhelpful thoughts associated with this stress. You might catch yourself thinking, "I'll never finish this project on time." Instead of identifying with this thought, you can view it as a thought, not a fact.

Finally, you can take values-based actions. If one of your core values is responsibility, you might choose to focus on the task at hand, prioritize effectively, and seek help if needed. By doing so, you're not avoiding the stress but managing it in a way that aligns with your values and serves your well-being.

Navigating Office Politics

With its complex network of alliances, conflicts, and power dynamics, office politics can often seem like a minefield. Emotional agility can serve as a compass, guiding us through this minefield with integrity and respect.

Consider a situation where you're caught in a power struggle between two senior colleagues. You might feel torn between supporting one over the other. Instead of reacting impulsively, you can choose to acknowledge your emotions. You might feel conflicted, anxious, or even frustrated.

Then, you can detach from any unhelpful thoughts. For example, you might find yourself thinking, "I have to pick a side." Observe this thought and question its validity. Are there other options you could consider?

Following this, you can focus on values-based actions. If fairness and respect are among your core values, you might decide to remain neutral, treat both colleagues respectfully, and focus on your tasks. This approach helps you navigate office politics effectively, aligns with your values, and fosters a sense of authenticity.

Managing Work-Life Balance

The scales of work-life balance can often tip toward the work side, leaving us scrambling to regain equilibrium. Emotional agility can help us restore this balance, ensuring we balance our professional responsibilities and personal well-being.

Imagine you're working late hours consistently, leaving little time for relaxation or personal activities. You might feel exhausted and overwhelmed. Emotional agility invites you to acknowledge these feelings without judgment.

Next, you can detach from unhelpful thoughts. For example, you might think, "I have to work hard to be successful." Observe this thought and question its validity. Does success always require sacrificing personal well-being?

Finally, you can take values-based actions. Suppose work-life balance is one of your core values. In that case, you might decide to set boundaries for your work hours, make time for relaxation and personal activities, and communicate your needs to your supervisor. These actions help restore work-life balance, align with your values, and enhance your overall well-being.

In the vibrant tapestry of the corporate world, emotional agility shines as a vital thread. It intertwines with the challenges of workplace stress, office politics, and work-life balance, transforming them into opportunities for growth and well-being. Applying emotional agility in these scenarios enhances our professional lives and enriches our emotional intelligence, paving the way for a more balanced, fulfilling life.

8.4 EMOTIONAL AGILITY SUCCESS STORY: A PERSONAL ACCOUNT

Personal Story of Achieving Emotional Agility

Let us turn our attention to the life of Richard, a high-powered attorney renowned for his sharp intellect and relentless ambition. Richard thrived in the cutthroat world of corporate law, a world where emotions were considered a liability rather than an asset. Over time, however, the constant suppression of his feelings began to take a toll on Richard. He was caught in a whirlpool of stress, frustration, and emotional exhaustion. He realized that his emotional rigidity was not only affecting his mental health but also his relationships and job satisfaction.

This realization sparked a transformation in Richard. He decided to cultivate emotional agility, shifting from an emotionally rigid mindset to a flexible, adaptive one. Richard began to acknowledge his emotions, labeling them without judgment. He allowed himself to feel stress, frustration, and even fear, understanding that these feelings were natural responses to his high-stress work environment.

Challenges Faced and Overcome

Richard's path to emotional agility was strewn with challenges. He grappled with self-doubt and resistance, especially in the early stages of his transformation. His high-stress job left him with little time for introspection and emotional self-care. Moreover, his years of emotional suppression had created a deep-seated habit of ignoring his feelings, a habit that was hard to break.

However, Richard was not deterred by these challenges. He sought the help of a psychologist, who introduced him to mindfulness techniques and helped him understand the concept of emotional agility. He started practicing mindfulness meditation, focusing on his breath and observing his thoughts and emotions without judgment. He learned to detach from unhelpful thoughts, viewing them as passing clouds in the sky of his mind rather than absolute truths.

Richard also started taking values-based actions. He identified his core values: integrity, respect, and balance. He began to make choices and take actions aligned with these values, even in the face of challenging emotions. For instance, when he felt stressed about a looming deadline, he chose to take a short break to practice mindfulness because one of his core values was balance.

Lessons Learned and Insights Gained

Over time, Richard noticed a significant shift in his emotional landscape. He was no longer at the mercy of his emotions but could navigate them with flexibility and understanding. He found himself handling work stress more effectively, leading with empathy, and experiencing enhanced job satisfaction. His relationships improved, as he was now able to understand and share the feelings of others. His overall mental health improved, as he was no longer suppressing his emotions but acknowledging and managing them effectively.

Richard's transformation from emotional rigidity to emotional agility is a testament to the transformative power of emotional intelligence. His story highlights the importance of acknowledging and labeling emotions, detaching from unhelpful thoughts, and taking values-based actions. It shows that emotional agility can be cultivated, leading to enhanced mental health, improved relationships, and greater job satisfaction.

Richard's story serves as an inspiration for all of us. It reminds us that we can cultivate emotional agility no matter how rigid our emotional patterns may be. It encourages us to embrace our emotions, dance with them, and use them to guide our journey toward emotional intelligence.

EMOTIONAL INTELLIGENCE FOR BETTER RELATIONSHIPS

Imagine being in a room full of people, yet feeling utterly alone—surrounded by chatter and laughter but drowned in silence. The world of relationships can often seem like this paradoxical room filled with joy, sorrow, connection, disconnection, understanding, and confusion. As social beings, we yearn to build strong, fulfilling relationships with our partners, friends, or family members. However, the path to such relationships is often strewn with emotional hurdles—misunderstandings, conflicts, and unmet expectations. What if I told you that emotional intelligence could be your guide on this path, helping you navigate these hurdles and build harmonious relationships?

Emotional intelligence, with its focus on self-awareness, emotional regulation, and empathy, plays a pivotal role in our relationships. It's like a compass, guiding us through the complex maze of human emotions, ensuring we don't lose our way in the twists and turns of misunderstandings or conflicts. In this chapter, we will explore the dynamics of emotional intelligence in romantic relationships, friendships, and family relationships.

9.1 RELATIONSHIP DYNAMICS: THE ROLE OF EMOTIONAL INTELLIGENCE

Emotional Intelligence in Romantic Relationships

Romantic relationships, with their intricate blend of love, passion, and commitment, are often the most emotionally intense relationships we experience. Emotional intelligence is crucial in these relationships, enhancing intimacy, fostering understanding, and resolving conflicts.

Consider the scenario of a heated argument with your partner. Your partner is upset about something you did, and you're feeling defensive. Here's where emotional intelligence comes into play. Self-awareness allows you to recognize your feelings of defensiveness and your partner's upset. Emotional regulation helps you manage your defensive reaction, preventing the argument from escalating. Empathy allows you to understand your partner's feelings from their perspective, enhancing mutual understanding.

Applying emotional intelligence in romantic relationships can foster a deeper emotional connection, manage conflicts effectively, and enhance overall satisfaction.

Emotional Intelligence in Friendships

Friendships, the ties that bind us beyond familial bonds and romantic connections, hold a special place in our lives. They offer support, companionship, and shared joy. In this context, emotional intelligence enhances empathy, facilitates effective communication, and fosters mutual understanding.

Imagine a situation where your friend is sharing a problem they're facing. Emotional intelligence can guide your response. Self-awareness would help you recognize your feelings about the problem. Emotional regulation would prevent these feelings from overshadowing your friend's emotions. Empathy would enable you to understand your friend's feelings and respond with compassion and support.

Applying emotional intelligence in friendships can deepen emotional connections, improve communication, and strengthen the bond of friendship.

Emotional Intelligence in Family Relationships

Family relationships, often characterized by deep emotional bonds and long-standing patterns of interaction, can be a complex emotional landscape to navigate. Emotional intelligence plays a vital role in these relationships, promoting empathy, enhancing communication, and fostering emotional well-being.

Consider a typical family dinner, a scenario familiar to most of us. The conversation flows along with the dishes, sprinkled with laughter, casual updates, and occasional disagreements. Emotional intelligence can enhance the experience of these family interactions. Self-awareness would help you recognize your emotions in response to the conversation. Emotional regulation would enable you to manage your emotional responses effectively. Empathy would allow you to understand your family members' perspectives, promoting mutual understanding and respect.

Incorporating emotional intelligence in family relationships can foster a positive family environment, enhance mutual understanding, and improve overall family well-being.

The dynamics of emotional intelligence in romantic relationships, friendships, and family relationships underscore its significance in enhancing our social and emotional lives. By recognizing our emotions, managing them effectively, and understanding others' emotions, we can build fulfilling relationships characterized by mutual understanding, effective communication, and deep emotional connections. As we navigate the complex landscape of human relationships, emotional intelligence is our compass, guiding us toward emotional harmony and social well-being.

9.2 EMOTIONAL INTELLIGENCE TECHNIQUES FOR HARMONIOUS RELATIONSHIPS

Active Listening

The Power of Presence

Consider for a moment the last conversation you had. Were you truly present, fully focused on the words and emotions of the person speaking to you? Or were you partially distracted, your mind drifting to your to-do list, worries, or responses? Active listening, a vital facet of emotional intelligence, is about immersing yourself completely in the conversation, focusing on the spoken words and underlying emotions.

The Art of Engagement

Active listening is an engaging process. It's about maintaining eye contact, responding with appropriate expressions, and offering verbal affirmations. When you nod in agreement, maintain receptive body language, or offer a simple "I see," you signal to the speaker that you're fully engaged in the conversation.

The Gift of Understanding

Yet active listening goes beyond these physical cues. It's about understanding the speaker's perspective, recognizing their emotions, and responding empathetically. It's about refraining from interruption or judgment and allowing the speaker to express their thoughts and feelings freely.

Incorporating active listening into our conversations can enhance mutual understanding, foster emotional connections, and contribute to harmonious relationships. It's a skill that requires practice, but the results are well worth the effort.

Expressing Emotions Effectively

The Language of Emotions

Emotions are our internal compass, guiding us through the terrain of our experiences. They are our body's way of communicating with us, signaling when we're happy, sad, angry, or afraid. Yet, expressing these emotions can be challenging for many of us. Emotional intelligence gives us the tools to express our emotions effectively, enhancing our relationships.

The Art of Expression

Expressing emotions effectively involves being aware of our feelings, understanding them, and conveying them respectfully and assertively. It's about saying, "I feel upset when you cancel our plans at the last minute," instead of, "You always ruin everything." It's about expressing our feelings without blaming, criticizing, or attacking the other person.

The Gift of Authenticity

The ability to express our emotions effectively allows us to be authentic in our relationships. It invites open and honest communication, reduces misunderstandings, and fosters mutual respect. Whether with our partners, friends, or family members, effectively expressing our emotions can enhance the quality of our interactions and the depth of our connections.

Resolving Conflicts Constructively

The Reality of Conflicts

Conflicts, like the changing seasons, are inevitable in our relationships. They arise from differences in opinions, clashes in personalities, or discrepancies in expectations. While conflicts can be challenging, they also offer opportunities for growth, understanding, and relationship enhancement. Emotional intelligence guides us in resolving conflicts constructively, turning potential roadblocks into bridges of understanding.

The Art of Resolution

Resolving conflicts constructively involves recognizing our emotions and those of the other person, managing these emotions effectively, and seeking a resolution that respects the needs and feelings of all parties involved. It's about taking a step back during a heated argument, taking a few deep breaths, and addressing the issue calmly and respectfully. It's about finding a middle ground where both parties feel heard, understood, and valued.

The Gift of Harmony

Conflict resolution, guided by emotional intelligence, can restore harmony in our relationships. It can clear misunderstandings, facilitate open communication, and foster mutual understanding. By resolving conflicts constructively, we can enhance our relationships, making them more resilient, harmonious, and fulfilling.

In the intricate dance of relationships, emotional intelligence is our dance partner, guiding our steps, matching our rhythm, and turning potential missteps into graceful twirls. As we practice active listening, express our emotions effectively, and resolve conflicts constructively, we enhance our emotional intelligence, enrich our relationships, and navigate the dance floor of human interaction with grace and confidence.

9.3 HANDLING DIFFICULT PEOPLE WITH EMOTIONAL INTELLIGENCE

Setting Boundaries

In relationships, boundaries represent invisible lines that define how we allow others to influence our thoughts, feelings, and actions. They are the safeguards that protect our emotional space from being infringed upon or violated. Emotional intelligence empowers us to set and maintain these boundaries effectively, particularly when dealing with difficult people.

Picture yourself in a situation where a colleague consistently undermines your ideas in team meetings. Emotional intelligence would guide you to recognize and validate your feelings of frustration. It would then prompt you to set a boundary by respectfully expressing your concern to the colleague or discussing the issue with your supervisor. By setting this boundary, you assert your self-respect, maintain your emotional well-being, and contribute to a healthier work environment.

Responding Instead of Reacting

In the heat of the moment, especially when dealing with difficult people, we may find ourselves reacting impulsively, driven by the intensity of our emotions. Emotional intelligence, however, encourages us to respond rather than react. This involves acknowledging our emotions, managing them effectively, and then choosing a response that aligns with our values and serves our well-being.

Imagine a situation where a friend repeatedly cancels plans at the last minute, leaving you feeling disappointed and disrespected. A reaction might be to confront the friend angrily or to retaliate by canceling plans arbitrarily. A response guided by emotional intelligence would involve recognizing your disappointment and disrespect, managing these emotions effectively, and then expressing your feelings to your friend calmly and respectfully. By choosing to respond instead of react, you address the issue constructively, fostering understanding and respect in the relationship.

Seeking Win-Win Solutions

Emotional intelligence equips us to manage our emotions and actions and guides us to seek solutions that benefit all parties involved. It encourages us to shift our perspective from a win-lose scenario to a win-win scenario, fostering cooperation, mutual respect, and positive relationship dynamics.

Consider a situation where you and your partner disagree on how to spend a shared holiday. You might prefer a relaxing beach vacation, while your partner might prefer an adventurous mountain trek. Instead of insisting on your preference, emotional intelligence would prompt you to seek a win-win solution. You might suggest spending a few days on the beach and a few days in the mountains, thereby respecting both your preferences and fostering mutual satisfaction.

Emotional intelligence guides our interactions with difficult people by illuminating the path toward constructive communication, mutual respect, and positive relationship dynamics. By setting boundaries, choosing to respond instead of reacting, and seeking win-win solutions, we can navigate the complexities of these interactions with confidence, respect, and emotional balance.

9.4 RELATIONSHIP TRANSFORMATION: AN EMOTIONAL INTELLIGENCE SUCCESS STORY

Sophia's story encapsulates emotional intelligence's transformative power in enhancing relationships.

Personal Story of Relationship Improvement

Sophia, a brilliant scientist, was known for her groundbreaking research and relentless dedication to her work. Yet, when it came to her personal relationships, she often found herself at a loss. She struggled to connect with her colleagues personally, and her friendships seemed to skim the surface, lacking depth and intimacy. Most significantly, her relationship with her partner, although filled with love and respect, was marked with frequent misunderstandings and conflicts.

The turning point came when Sophia chanced upon a book on emotional intelligence. Intrigued by the concept, she decided to delve deeper. As she learned about self-awareness, emotional regulation, and empathy, she realized that these were the missing pieces in her relationship puzzle. She decided to cultivate these skills, hoping to enhance her personal relationships and achieve emotional balance.

Role of Emotional Intelligence in Transformation

Sophia's journey toward emotional intelligence was marked by self-reflection, conscious practice, and gradual transformation. She started with introspection, trying to understand her emotions and how they influenced her actions. She then began to manage her emotions more effectively, preventing them from spiraling out of control during stressful situations or heated arguments.

The most significant shift, however, came when she began to practice empathy. She started listening more attentively, not just to the words spoken by others but also to the emotions underlying those words. She learned to step into their shoes, see the world from their perspective, and respond with understanding and compassion.

This transformation was not overnight but gradual and steady. Each step she took toward emotional intelligence brought her closer to a deeper understanding of herself and others. Each skill she cultivated added a new dimension to her relationships, enhancing their depth and harmony.

Key Takeaways and Lessons Learned

Over time, Sophia began to notice changes in her relationships. Her conversations with her colleagues went beyond work, delving into personal interests and shared experiences. Her friendships deepened, marked by emotional connections and mutual understanding. Most significantly, her relationship with her partner improved. Their conflicts reduced, their communication improved, and their bond deepened.

Sophia's transformation is a testament to the power of emotional intelligence in enhancing relationships. Her story offers valuable insights and lessons for all of us:

1. Self-awareness is the starting point of emotional intelligence. By understanding our emotions, we can manage them more effectively, preventing them from adversely affecting our relationships.
2. Emotional regulation is vital to maintaining harmony in relationships. It allows us to respond to conflicts and

disagreements in a calm and balanced manner, fostering understanding and respect.
3. Empathy bridges the gap between individuals, fostering emotional connection and mutual understanding. By practicing empathy, we can enhance the depth and quality of our relationships.

Sophia's story is a shining thread in the tapestry of human relationships, reminding us of the transformative power of emotional intelligence. It celebrates our potential to enhance our relationships, foster deeper connections, and live a life marked by emotional harmony and understanding. As we move forward, let's carry these insights with us, each step taking us closer to the world of emotional intelligence and echoing with the rhythm of Sophia's transformative dance.

In the following chapters, we will continue to explore the multifaceted world of emotional intelligence. We will delve into its application in various aspects of life, from parenting to workplace dynamics, from mental health to personal growth. As we do so, let's remember Sophia's story, let it inspire us, and let it guide us on our path toward emotional intelligence.

EMOTIONAL INTELLIGENCE: YOUR HIDDEN SUPERPOWER AT WORK

Have you ever wondered what propels some individuals to the pinnacle of career success while others, seemingly equally competent, remain stuck in mediocrity? Is it intelligence, technical skills, or sheer luck? While these factors certainly play a role, the secret ingredient to career success often lies in an overlooked and undervalued skill—emotional intelligence. In the bustling corridors of the corporate world, where stress is high and competition fierce, emotional intelligence emerges as a hidden superpower that can significantly impact your career trajectory.

10.1 THE IMPACT OF EMOTIONAL INTELLIGENCE ON CAREER SUCCESS

Emotional Intelligence and Leadership

"Leadership is not about being in charge. It's about taking care of those in your charge," says Simon Sinek, renowned leadership expert. This statement emphasizes the heart of leadership—people.

At its core, leadership is about understanding, motivating, and guiding people toward a common goal. And this is where emotional intelligence comes into play.

Emotionally intelligent leaders are adept at recognizing and understanding their emotions and those of their team members. This self-awareness and empathy allow them to tap into the emotional undercurrents that drive their team's behavior and performance. They can sense the team's morale, anticipate emotional responses, and adjust their leadership approach accordingly.

Moreover, emotionally intelligent leaders are skilled at emotional regulation. They can manage their emotions, even in stressful situations, modeling emotional stability and resilience for their team. This ability to stay calm under pressure fosters a positive work environment and enhances the team's morale and productivity.

Finally, emotionally intelligent leaders excel in interpersonal relationships. They communicate effectively, resolve conflicts constructively, and build strong, positive relationships with their team members. This ability to connect with others on an emotional level fosters trust and cooperation, enhancing team cohesion and performance.

In essence, emotional intelligence can significantly enhance leadership effectiveness, contributing to team performance, job satisfaction, and organizational success.

Emotional Intelligence and Teamwork

Teamwork is like a symphony. It's not about playing the loudest or the fastest but about playing in harmony with others. Emotional intelligence is the maestro that can orchestrate this harmony.

Emotionally intelligent team members contribute to effective teamwork in several ways. They are adept at recognizing and understanding their own and their teammates' emotions. This emotional awareness enables them to navigate the emotional dynamics within the team, fostering a positive team climate.

Moreover, emotionally intelligent team members excel at emotional regulation. They can effectively manage their emotions, preventing emotional outbursts or conflicts that disrupt team harmony.

Additionally, emotionally intelligent team members are skilled at empathetic communication. They can understand and share the feelings of their teammates, fostering mutual respect and understanding. This empathetic communication can enhance team cohesion, facilitating effective collaboration and team performance.

In brief, emotional intelligence can significantly enhance teamwork, contributing to team cohesion, performance, and job satisfaction.

Emotional Intelligence and Job Satisfaction

Job satisfaction is like a puzzle. It's not just about the size or the picture on the box but about how well the pieces fit together. Emotional intelligence is the tool that can help us assemble this puzzle effectively.

Emotionally intelligent individuals derive greater satisfaction from their jobs. They are better equipped to manage work-related stress, navigate workplace relationships, and align their work with their values.

Moreover, emotionally intelligent individuals are more engaged in their work. They are attuned to their emotions and can channel their emotional energy to enhance their performance and productivity.

Finally, emotionally intelligent individuals are more resilient and can bounce back from setbacks and failures. This resilience can contribute to a positive attitude toward work, enhancing job satisfaction.

In conclusion, emotional intelligence can significantly enhance job satisfaction, contributing to work engagement, resilience, and overall well-being at work.

10.2 TECHNIQUES TO APPLY EMOTIONAL INTELLIGENCE AT WORK

Building Positive Relationships

In the interconnected web of the professional arena, each thread represents a relationship woven together to form the fabric of our work life. Emotional intelligence forms the loom that weaves these threads together, fostering positive relationships at work.

The first step to building these relationships is to exercise empathy. This involves genuinely understanding the feelings and perspectives of your colleagues and fostering a sense of mutual respect. For instance, if a team member is struggling with a task, an empathetic approach would be to offer help or advice rather than blaming them for slowing the team down.

Next, effective communication is vital. This involves clearly expressing your thoughts and feelings and actively listening to others. For example, if you disagree with a point made in a meeting, articulate your differing viewpoint respectfully, ensuring your tone and body language are non-confrontational.

Finally, fostering a positive environment is essential. This can be achieved by acknowledging others' efforts, celebrating team successes, and maintaining a positive attitude, even when faced with challenges.

Managing Workplace Stress

Like a looming storm cloud, workplace stress can often cast a shadow over our professional lives. Emotional intelligence, however, can serve as the silver lining, enabling us to manage this stress effectively.

To begin with, it's crucial to recognize the signs of stress, such as feeling overwhelmed, irritability, or difficulty concentrating. Acknowledging these signs is the first step toward managing workplace stress.

Next, implementing stress management techniques can be beneficial. These may include deep breathing exercises, taking regular breaks, or engaging in physical activity. For instance, if you're feeling stressed due to an approaching deadline, taking a short walk or practicing a few minutes of mindful breathing can help reduce stress levels.

Lastly, maintaining a balanced perspective is key. This involves viewing challenges as opportunities for growth rather than threats. It also means maintaining a healthy work-life balance, ensuring that work pressures do not infringe on personal time and well-being.

Leading with Empathy

In its truest sense, leadership is about influencing others through understanding and inspiration rather than authority or coercion. Emotional intelligence forms the cornerstone of such leadership, with empathy playing a pivotal role.

To lead with empathy, it's essential to understand the feelings and perspectives of your team members. This involves listening to their concerns, acknowledging their feelings, and appreciating their efforts. For example, before implementing a major change, seek feedback from your team and consider their viewpoints.

Next, demonstrating emotional transparency is essential. This involves sharing your feelings and concerns with your team and fostering an environment of trust and openness. However, it's crucial to balance transparency with professionalism, ensuring that emotional sharing does not cross professional boundaries.

Finally, it is key to make decisions that consider the team's emotional well-being. This involves assessing the emotional impact of decisions and, where possible, involving the team in decision-making processes. This fosters a sense of ownership and involvement among team members and leads to decisions that are more considerate of everyone's emotional well-being.

10.3 HANDLING WORKPLACE STRESS WITH EMOTIONAL INTELLIGENCE

Recognizing Stress Triggers

In the realm of the corporate landscape, stress is an all too familiar companion. Like a chameleon, it changes hues, manifesting in various forms such as looming deadlines, high workloads, or interpersonal conflicts. Emotional intelligence arms us with a discerning lens, allowing us to identify these stress triggers before they escalate into overwhelming stress.

Identifying stress triggers begins with a heightened sense of self-awareness. Tuning into our emotional state throughout the day can provide valuable clues about potential stress triggers. For example, if you notice a spike in anxiety each time a particular manager assigns you a task, the interaction with this manager could be a stress trigger.

Keeping a stress journal can also be an effective strategy for recognizing stress triggers. Noting down instances when you felt stressed, including the situation, your thoughts, and your emotional response, can help identify patterns over time. It's like piecing together a puzzle; each entry adds a piece, and over time, a clearer picture of your stress triggers begins to emerge.

Using Mindfulness to Manage Stress

Once we've identified the triggers, the next step is managing the stress they induce. This is where mindfulness, a key element of emotional intelligence, steps in. Mindfulness is about being fully present in the moment, observing our thoughts, feelings, and sensations without judgment.

When stress levels start to rise, a simple mindfulness technique can be to pause and take a few deep breaths. This act of mindful breathing can help to interrupt the stress response, providing a calming influence. It's like hitting the "reset" button, allowing space for a more considered response to the situation.

Another useful mindfulness technique is the "body scan." This involves mentally scanning your body from head to toe and observing any sensations or tensions. During moments of stress, bodily tensions often increase. The body scan technique allows you to become aware of these tensions and consciously relax your body, which in turn can help to reduce feelings of stress.

Building Resilience at Work

Building resilience, the ability to bounce back from adversity is like donning armor that shields us from the negative impacts of workplace stress. It's about developing the capacity to weather the storms of stress and emerge more robust and better equipped to handle future stressors.

One way to build resilience is by practicing cognitive reframing. This involves shifting our perspective of a stressful situation, viewing it as a challenge to overcome rather than a threat. So, if you're feeling stressed about a looming deadline, instead of thinking, "I'll never get this done on time, and I'll fail," you could reframe it to, "This is a challenge, but I have faced and overcome similar ones before."

Maintaining a balanced lifestyle is another critical aspect of building resilience. Ensuring regular periods of rest and relaxation, engaging in physical activity, and nurturing social connections can all contribute to resilience. These elements act as a counterbalance to stress, replenishing our emotional resources and equipping us to handle future stressors better.

Developing a growth mindset, the belief that abilities and intelligence can be developed, is also a powerful tool for building resilience. With a growth mindset, setbacks or failures are viewed as opportunities for learning and growth, fostering resilience.

While stress is a common phenomenon in the workplace, it doesn't have to be a career-derailing force. By recognizing stress triggers, practicing mindfulness techniques, and building resilience, you can harness the power of emotional intelligence to manage workplace stress effectively. This proactive approach to stress management can lead to improved performance, healthier work relationships, and increased job satisfaction.

Emotional intelligence, therefore, serves as a critical tool in our professional toolkit, enabling us to navigate workplace stress and enhance our career success. As we continue to hone our emotional intelligence skills, we are better equipped to thrive in the corporate world, turning the challenges we face into stepping stones for growth and success.

10.4 WORKPLACE VICTORY: AN EMOTIONAL INTELLIGENCE CASE STUDY

Personal Story of Workplace Success

Meet Laura, a dynamic, passionate, and ambitious marketing executive working at a fast-paced tech firm. Known for her relentless drive and strategic prowess, Laura was a rising star in her organization. However, despite her impressive professional accomplishments, Laura found herself grappling with mounting stress, volatile emotions, and dwindling job satisfaction.

A high-stakes project that Laura was leading had hit a roadblock. The client was unhappy, the team was demotivated, and the deadline was fast approaching. Laura felt a tremendous amount of pressure and began to doubt her abilities. She was on the brink of burnout.

Then, Laura attended a workshop on emotional intelligence. It was a revelation. She realized that while she had been focusing on honing her technical and strategic skills, she had neglected the equally crucial aspect of managing her emotions. Intrigued by the potential of emotional intelligence to transform her work experience, Laura decided to cultivate it.

Role of Emotional Intelligence in Career Advancement

Laura began cultivating her emotional intelligence by practicing mindfulness. She would start each day with a few minutes of mindful breathing, tuning into her emotions, and setting a positive intention for the day. This practice helped Laura to start each day with a calm and focused mind, enhancing her productivity.

Next, Laura worked on improving her emotional regulation. She learned to identify when her emotions were escalating and used mindfulness techniques to manage her responses. This skill proved particularly useful during stressful meetings or difficult conversations. Laura was able to stay calm, respond thoughtfully, and manage conflicts more effectively.

Laura also focused on enhancing her empathy. She made a conscious effort to understand her team members' perspectives and emotions, which improved team cohesion and morale. Laura's empathetic leadership style fostered a positive work environment, leading to improved team performance and client satisfaction.

These changes did not go unnoticed. Laura's improved leadership skills, coupled with her continued excellence in strategic planning and execution, led to her promotion to Marketing Director. This was a testament to the power of emotional intelligence in accelerating career advancement.

Lessons Learned and Insights Gained

Laura's transformation underlines the significant impact emotional intelligence can have on our careers. Here are some key insights gleaned from Laura's experience:

1. Mindfulness Matters: Starting the day with mindfulness can set a positive tone for the rest of the day, enhancing focus, productivity, and overall job satisfaction.
2. Emotion Regulation Is Key: Being able to manage our emotions, particularly in stressful situations, can significantly improve our professional relationships and performance.
3. Empathy Enhances Leadership: Understanding and sharing the feelings of our team members can foster a positive work environment, enhance team performance, and improve leadership effectiveness.

Laura's story serves as an inspiration for all of us. It shows that no matter how challenging our work environment may be, we have the power to transform it by cultivating emotional intelligence. It's a reminder that our emotions are not our enemies but powerful allies that can propel us toward career success and personal fulfillment when understood and managed effectively.

As we continue our exploration of emotional intelligence, let's carry these insights with us. Let's remember that our emotions, when harnessed with intelligence, can become our most potent superpower, enabling us to soar to new heights in our careers, our relationships, and our lives. As we turn the page to the next chapter, we will explore how emotional intelligence plays a vital role in the most rewarding and challenging role many of us will undertake—parenting.

EMOTIONAL INTELLIGENCE: NURTURING THE HEART OF PARENTING

Imagine the role of a parent as a skilled gardener, nurturing the tender saplings of their child's emotional landscape. The gardener ensures that the saplings receive adequate sunshine, water, and nourishment, facilitating their growth into strong, resilient trees. As parents, we undertake a similar role, nurturing our children's emotional growth and ensuring they develop into emotionally intelligent, resilient individuals. Emotional intelligence, with its focus on self-awareness, emotional regulation, and empathy, serves as the sunshine, water, and nourishment in this nurturing process.

In the realm of parenting, emotional intelligence holds a pivotal role. It's the key that unlocks deeper bonds with our children, fosters their emotional and social development, and guides them toward a resilient, fulfilling life. The importance of emotional intelligence in parenting extends across various dimensions—child development, parent-child bonding, and child behavior.

11.1 THE IMPORTANCE OF EMOTIONAL INTELLIGENCE IN PARENTING

Emotional Intelligence and Child Development

Just as the roots of a tree are critical for its growth and stability, emotional intelligence forms the foundational roots of a child's overall development. It influences various aspects of a child's cognitive, social, and emotional growth.

Cognitive development, which involves thinking, learning, and problem-solving skills, is significantly influenced by emotional intelligence. For example, a child who is adept at recognizing and managing emotions can better focus on tasks, enhancing his or her learning and problem-solving abilities.

Social development, which involves interactions and relationships with others, is also closely linked with emotional intelligence. Children with high emotional intelligence can understand and manage their own emotions and those of others, enhancing their social interactions and relationships.

Finally, emotional intelligence plays a crucial role in a child's emotional development. It helps children understand and manage their feelings, fostering emotional stability and well-being. For instance, a child who can recognize feelings of anger and calm down before acting on these feelings exhibits emotional intelligence.

Emotional Intelligence and Parent-Child Bonding

Consider the parent-child relationship as a dance duet. The harmony and rhythm of the dance rely on the emotional connection between the dancers. Emotional intelligence serves as the rhythm that syncs the dance steps, enhancing the parent-child bond.

Parents who exhibit emotional intelligence are more attuned to their child's emotions. They can understand and validate these emotions, fostering a sense of emotional safety for the child. This emotional attunement enhances the parent-child bond, making the child feel understood and valued.

Moreover, emotionally intelligent parents can effectively manage their own emotions, modeling emotional regulation for their children. This emotional balance prevents parenting stress from spilling over into the parent-child relationship, further enhancing the emotional bond.

Emotional Intelligence and Child Behavior

Emotional intelligence is a compass that guides a child's behavior. It influences how a child reacts to situations, manages impulses, and interacts with others.

Children with high emotional intelligence can recognize and manage their emotions, resulting in more positive behavior. For example, a child who can recognize feelings of frustration and use calming strategies is less likely to have an outburst.

Additionally, emotional intelligence enhances a child's social behavior. Children who understand their own and others' emotions can navigate social situations more effectively. They can exhibit empathy, manage conflicts, and foster positive relationships.

In essence, emotional intelligence holds profound significance in parenting. It influences a child's development, fosters a strong parent-child bond, and guides their behavior. As parents, nurturing emotional intelligence is akin to nurturing the heart of our child's emotional, social, and cognitive growth. It's about equipping our children with the emotional skills they need to navigate the journey of life with resilience, empathy, and fulfillment.

11.2 EMOTIONAL INTELLIGENCE TECHNIQUES FOR EFFECTIVE PARENTING

Emotion Coaching: Guiding the Emotional Journey of Childhood

Emotion coaching is a technique that lies at the heart of effective parenting. This process involves helping your child understand their emotions, guiding them to manage these feelings, and teaching them to respond to emotional situations in a healthy manner.

When your child experiences an emotional situation, the first step in emotion coaching is to tune into your child's feelings. This could involve observing their body language, listening to their words, or simply acknowledging the emotional context of the situation. For instance, if your child has just lost a game and looks upset, recognizing this emotion forms the first step in emotion coaching.

Next, validate their feelings. Let them know it's perfectly fine to feel upset about losing. This validation communicates that their feelings are important and acceptable, fostering emotional safety and self-acceptance.

Following validation, help your child label their emotions. This could involve saying something like, "It seems like you're feeling really disappointed about losing the game." Labeling emotions enhances emotional awareness and provides a vocabulary for expressing feelings.

Then, guide your child in managing their emotions. This could involve suggesting calming techniques, such as deep breathing or taking a quiet break. It's also important to teach them that while they cannot control the situation (in this case, losing the game), they can control their response to it.

Finally, help your child problem-solve. This might involve discussing what they could do differently in the next game or how they can handle similar situations in the future. This will equip the child with problem-solving skills and foster resilience as they learn to view challenges as opportunities for learning and growth.

Modeling Emotional Intelligence: Leading by Example

As parents, we are our children's first and most influential teachers. Children learn more from what we do than what we say. Therefore, modeling emotional intelligence can be a powerful tool for teaching these skills to our children.

Modeling emotional intelligence involves demonstrating self-awareness, emotional regulation, and empathy in our day-to-day interactions. It's about showing our children how we recognize, understand, and manage our emotions.

For example, if you're feeling frustrated about a work issue, you might say to your child, "I'm feeling a bit frustrated right now because something didn't go as planned at work. I think I'll take a few deep breaths to help me calm down." This not only models emotional awareness and regulation but also communicates that talking about our emotions is okay.

Similarly, showing empathy in your interactions with your child and others can teach them the importance of understanding and sharing the feelings of others. For instance, if your child is upset about a friend moving away, you could say, "I understand that you're feeling sad because you'll miss your friend. It's okay to feel this way."

Encouraging Emotional Expression: Fostering an Open Emotional Climate

Encouraging emotional expression in your child is like opening the windows in a stuffy room. It allows emotions to flow freely, preventing emotional bottlenecks and fostering emotional well-being.

Creating an open emotional climate at home is key to encouraging emotional expression. This involves making it clear that all emotions, whether positive or negative, are accepted and respected. It's about providing a safe space for your child to express their emotions without fear of judgment or dismissal.

You can encourage emotional expression by inviting your child to share their feelings regularly. This could be during quiet moments like bedtime or day-to-day activities like driving to school. Asking open-ended questions like "How did you feel when that happened?" or "What do you think about that?" can facilitate emotional expression.

Remember, encouraging emotional expression is not about prying or pushing your child to share. It's about creating an environment where emotions can be expressed freely and openly, fostering emotional intelligence, and enhancing your child's emotional well-being.

11.3 TEACHING KIDS EMOTIONAL INTELLIGENCE: PRACTICAL TIPS

Age-Appropriate Emotional Intelligence Activities

Developing emotional intelligence should start from an early age, and one of the most effective ways to do this is through age-appropriate activities. These activities should be fun, engaging, and tailored to your child's developmental stage.

For toddlers and preschoolers, simple games like "Guess the Emotion" can be a great start. In this game, parents can make various facial expressions and ask the child to identify the emotion. This helps young children to start recognizing and naming different emotions, a foundational skill in emotional intelligence.

As your child grows older and starts school, you can introduce more complex activities. Storytelling is a fantastic tool at this stage. Read stories with your child and discuss the characters' emotions. Ask questions like, "How do you think the character is feeling?" and "What would you feel if you were in the character's place?" This will enhance your child's understanding of emotions and help develop empathy.

For teenagers, activities can be more discussion-based. Encourage open conversations about emotions and how to manage them. Movies and books can serve as useful prompts for these discussions. Talk about the emotions portrayed by the characters, the consequences of their emotional responses, and how they could have managed their emotions differently.

Discussing Emotions Openly

Open discussions about emotions are vital in teaching kids emotional intelligence. These discussions can help children understand that all emotions, whether positive or negative, are normal and valid. It also provides them with a safe space to express their own emotions freely.

Start by sharing your own emotions with your child. For instance, if you've had a challenging day at work, you can say, "I felt really frustrated today because my project didn't go as planned." Sharing your own emotions not only normalizes emotional expression but also models how to talk about emotions.

Encourage your child to share their emotions, too. Ask them how they felt during various parts of their day, and listen attentively when they share. Validate their feelings and show empathy to make them feel heard and understood.

Remember to keep these discussions age-appropriate. Younger children may need more guidance and simpler language, while older children and teenagers may benefit from more in-depth discussions.

Encouraging Empathy and Understanding

Empathy, the ability to understand and share the feelings of others, is a crucial component of emotional intelligence. Encouraging empathy in children can help them build better relationships, respond to others' emotions appropriately, and become more socially aware.

One way to foster empathy is by modeling it. Show empathy in your interactions with others, and your child will learn from your example. If your child sees you responding to a friend's disappointment with understanding and comfort, they will learn to do the same.

Another effective approach is to discuss others' emotions with your child. For instance, if a sibling or a friend is upset, talk to your child about how that person might be feeling. Ask your child how they would feel in the same situation. This helps your child to put themselves in others' shoes and develop empathy.

Remember, teaching emotional intelligence is not a one-time lesson but a continuous process. It's about integrating these practices into your daily interactions with your child. Over time, these consistent efforts can help your child develop strong emotional intelligence skills that will benefit them in every aspect of their life.

11.4 PARENTING SUCCESS: AN EMOTIONAL INTELLIGENCE JOURNEY

Personal Story of Parenting Success

Meet Sarah, a dedicated high school teacher and a loving mother to an energetic nine-year-old, Emma. Sarah's days were a whirlwind of lesson planning, grading assignments, and parenting duties. Life was busy, but Sarah was managing it quite well, or so she thought. Over time, however, Sarah began to notice a shift in Emma's behavior. Emma, usually a happy and cooperative child, started having frequent meltdowns, became argumentative, and struggled with schoolwork. Sarah felt lost. She was adept at handling her students' needs but found herself struggling to navigate her own child's emotional turmoil.

Sarah's turning point came when she attended a workshop on emotional intelligence. The insights she gained about self-awareness, emotional regulation, and empathy were an eye-opener. She realized that while she was trying to fix Emma's behavior, she was missing the underlying emotions driving that behavior. Inspired, Sarah embarked on the path of integrating emotional intelligence into her parenting approach.

Role of Emotional Intelligence in Parenting Challenges

Sarah began by focusing on self-awareness, both her own and Emma's. She made a conscious effort to tune into her emotions during stressful parenting moments. Instead of reacting impulsively when Emma had a meltdown, Sarah paused to recognize her feelings of frustration. She then focused on understanding Emma's emotions, asking open-ended questions to help Emma express her feelings.

Emotional regulation was the next step. Sarah started practicing deep breathing exercises to manage her emotions during stressful parenting situations. She also taught these techniques to Emma, who began using them during her meltdowns.

Sarah also worked on enhancing empathy. She strived to understand Emma's perspective during conflicts, which often diffused tense situations. She also encouraged Emma to practice empathy with her friends, fostering her social-emotional development.

With these shifts, Sarah began to notice changes. Emma's meltdowns decreased, her behavior improved, and she seemed happier. Sarah, too, felt more confident and less stressed in her parenting. She felt more connected with Emma and found parenting to be more enjoyable and less of a struggle.

Key Takeaways and Lessons Learned

Sarah's experience offers valuable insights into the transformative power of emotional intelligence in parenting. Here are some key lessons from Sarah's story:

1. Understanding Emotions Is Key: Recognizing and understanding both our own and our child's emotions is the first step toward effective emotional intelligence-based parenting. This understanding can help us respond more effectively to our child's emotional needs.
2. Managing Our Emotions Helps Our Children Manage Theirs: Children learn more from what we do than what we say. We can teach our children to do the same by demonstrating effective emotional regulation.
3. Empathy Enhances Connection: Empathy can bridge the gap between misunderstanding and connection. By trying to understand our child's perspective, we can foster a stronger parent-child bond.

Sarah's story is a testament to the transformative power of emotional intelligence in parenting. It serves as a reminder that even when faced with parenting challenges, we have the tools to navigate them effectively. Emotional intelligence is one such tool, a guiding light that can illuminate our path, leading us to a more fulfilling and joyful parenting experience.

As we conclude this chapter, let's pause for a moment to reflect on the insights and lessons we have learned. Let's remember that we as parents have the power to nurture our children's emotional intelligence, shaping their emotional landscape for a resilient and fulfilling life.

In the coming chapter, we will explore another crucial facet of emotional intelligence—its impact on mental health. We'll delve into how emotional intelligence can enhance our psychological well-being and offer insights into managing anxiety, depression, and stress. As we turn the page, let's carry forward the lessons learned, ready to explore the intersection of emotional intelligence and mental health.

EMOTIONAL INTELLIGENCE: A BEACON OF LIGHT IN MENTAL HEALTH

Imagine standing at the shore during a stormy night, the sea raging with waves, the sky filled with tumultuous clouds. Amid this chaos, a lighthouse stands tall, its light cutting through the darkness, guiding seafarers safely to the shore. This is what emotional intelligence can be in the stormy seas of our mental health—a beacon of light guiding us toward emotional balance and psychological well-being.

The interplay between emotional intelligence and mental health is profound. Our ability to recognize, understand, manage, and utilize our emotions can significantly impact our mental health. It can shape our response to stress, influence our outlook on life, and enhance our psychological resilience. In this chapter, we will explore this vital interplay, focusing on three key aspects of mental health: anxiety, depression, and overall psychological well-being.

12.1 THE INTERPLAY BETWEEN EMOTIONAL INTELLIGENCE AND MENTAL HEALTH

Emotional Intelligence and Anxiety

Anxiety can feel like a whirlwind of worry, fear, and unease, often accompanied by physical symptoms such as rapid heart rate, sweating, or tremors. Emotional intelligence provides a grounding force in this whirlwind, helping us navigate through the storm of anxiety.

Self-awareness, a key component of emotional intelligence, enables us to recognize and understand our anxious feelings. By tuning into our emotions, we can identify triggers that escalate our anxiety and patterns that sustain it. For example, if giving presentations at work tends to spike your anxiety, recognizing this trigger can be the first step toward managing it.

Emotional regulation, another critical aspect of emotional intelligence, equips us with the skills to manage our anxiety effectively. Techniques such as deep breathing, progressive muscle relaxation, or cognitive reframing can help reduce the intensity of anxious feelings and bring about emotional balance.

Moreover, empathy, the ability to understand and share others' emotions, can help mitigate feelings of anxiety. Connecting with others who experience similar emotions can provide comfort, reduce feelings of isolation, and foster a sense of shared understanding.

Emotional Intelligence and Depression

Depression, characterized by pervasive feelings of sadness, loss of interest, and low energy, can feel like an endless tunnel of despair.

Emotional intelligence, however, can serve as a guiding light, leading the way toward hope and recovery.

Self-awareness helps us recognize our depressive feelings and understand their impact on our thoughts and behaviors. For instance, if you notice a pervasive sense of sadness and a loss of interest in activities you used to enjoy, recognizing these feelings can be the first step toward seeking help.

Emotional regulation provides us with strategies to manage depressive feelings. While it does not replace professional help, it can be a valuable adjunct to treatment. Techniques such as mindfulness, self-compassion, or positive affirmations can help shift our focus from negative to positive emotions, fostering emotional balance.

Empathy can play a significant role in managing depression. Connecting with others, understanding their struggles, and feeling understood can help alleviate feelings of loneliness often associated with depression.

Emotional Intelligence and Psychological Well-Being

Psychological well-being is like a serene lake, reflecting a sense of contentment, resilience, and emotional balance. Emotional intelligence serves as the nurturing rain that replenishes this lake, fostering psychological well-being.

Self-awareness cultivates psychological well-being by enhancing self-understanding and fostering authentic living. By recognizing and understanding our emotions, we can live in alignment with our true feelings and foster a sense of authenticity and well-being.

Emotional regulation contributes to psychological well-being by promoting emotional balance and resilience. By managing our emotions effectively, we can more easily navigate life's ups and downs, fostering resilience and well-being.

Empathy enhances psychological well-being by fostering connectedness and enhancing social relationships. By understanding and sharing others' emotions, we can build deeper connections and derive satisfaction from our social interactions, enhancing our psychological well-being.

In the realm of mental health, emotional intelligence empowers us to recognize and manage our emotions, empathize with others, and navigate the challenges of anxiety and depression. Cultivating emotional intelligence enriches our mental health, fostering resilience, contentment, and overall psychological well-being.

12.2 USING EMOTIONAL INTELLIGENCE TO MANAGE ANXIETY AND DEPRESSION

Recognizing and Accepting Emotions

In the battle against anxiety and depression, emotional intelligence is our shield and sword, protecting us and empowering us to fight back. Our first line of defense is the recognition and acceptance of our emotions. Consider this as the process of identifying the enemy and understanding its tactics. When anxiety or depression looms, our emotions often surge—fear, sadness, hopelessness. By using our emotional intelligence, we can identify these feelings, name them, and understand their triggers.

For instance, you might notice a creeping sense of dread each time you face a large audience or an overwhelming sadness that engulfs you during social gatherings. Recognizing these emotions and their triggers is the first step in managing them. However, recognition alone is not enough. It's equally important to accept and acknowledge these emotions without judgment or resistance. Remember, there's no shame in feeling anxious or depressed. These are human emotions shared by many. Accepting them reduces their power over us, paving the way for effective management.

Using Mindfulness to Manage Anxiety

Once we've recognized and accepted our emotions, we can then use the tool of mindfulness to manage anxiety. Mindfulness is like an anchor, keeping us grounded in the present moment and preventing us from being swept away by the stormy seas of anxiety. When anxious thoughts start racing through our minds, pulling us into a vortex of worry and fear, mindfulness brings us back to the present, to the here and now.

A simple mindfulness practice involves focusing on our breath. As anxiety surges, our breathing often becomes shallow and rapid. By deliberately slowing down our breath and taking deep and rhythmic breaths, we can counteract the physiological response to anxiety, calming our bodies and our minds. Each inhalation brings us life-giving oxygen, and each exhalation releases tension and fear, grounding us in the present moment.

Building Resilience to Overcome Depression

While mindfulness can help manage anxiety, building resilience is crucial in the fight against depression. Resilience is our emotional immune system, protecting us from the debilitating effects of depression and aiding in our recovery.

Building resilience starts with nurturing a positive mindset. It's about shifting our focus from what's wrong to what's right, from our flaws to our strengths, from our failures to our victories. Each time we encounter a failure or a setback, instead of succumbing to feelings of hopelessness or self-blame, we can view it as an opportunity for growth and learning. This shift in mindset not only fosters resilience but also instills a sense of hope, a belief that we can overcome the challenges we face.

Next, developing effective coping strategies is key to building resilience. These strategies might include engaging in physical activity, maintaining a balanced diet, getting adequate sleep, and seeking social support. Each of these strategies contributes to our physical and emotional well-being and enhances our capacity to bounce back from depression.

Lastly, seeking professional help is an integral part of building resilience. Depression is a serious mental health condition, and it's okay to seek help. A mental health professional can provide valuable guidance, therapeutic interventions, and medication if necessary. Seeking help is not a sign of weakness but a testament to our strength and our commitment to overcoming depression.

In the battle against anxiety and depression, emotional intelligence is our ally. It equips us with the recognition and acceptance of emotions, the practice of mindfulness, and the strength of resilience. Each of these tools empowers us to manage anxiety and depression, fostering emotional balance and psychological well-being.

12.3 EMOTIONAL INTELLIGENCE FOR IMPROVED PSYCHOLOGICAL WELL-BEING

Cultivating Positive Emotions

Emotional intelligence provides us with the tools to not only navigate the stormy seas of negative emotions but also to cultivate the serene waters of positive emotions. These positive emotions—joy, gratitude, contentment, inspiration, and pride, to name a few—can enhance our psychological well-being, acting as natural uplifts of the human spirit.

Picture your emotions as a garden. The negative emotions, like weeds, are often conspicuous, demanding your attention. Positive emotions, on the other hand, are like delicate buds that need nurturing. Emotional intelligence is the skilled gardener who knows how to manage the weeds and nurture the buds.

Self-awareness, a key component of emotional intelligence, enables us to recognize and savor positive emotions. Rejoicing in small victories, expressing gratitude for blessings, and deriving joy from simple pleasures are all ways to cultivate positive emotions in our daily lives.

Building Healthy Relationships

Humans are social beings, and our relationships significantly impact our psychological well-being. Emotional intelligence lays the foundation for building healthy relationships, enriching our social interactions, and enhancing our sense of belonging.

Think of your relationships as a dance. Emotional intelligence is the rhythm that syncs your steps with your partner's, creating a harmonious performance. Self-awareness helps you understand your needs and emotions in relationships. Emotional regulation enables you to manage disagreements and conflicts effectively. Empathy allows you to understand and share the feelings of others, fostering emotional intimacy.

Whether it's a close friendship, a romantic partnership, or a professional relationship, emotional intelligence can enhance the quality of our relationships, making them a source of joy, support, and fulfillment.

Achieving Work-Life Balance

In our fast-paced world, juggling work responsibilities and personal life can often feel like walking a tightrope. Emotional intelligence can provide the balance we need to walk this tightrope effectively, enhancing our work-life balance and, consequently, our psychological well-being.

Imagine your work and personal life as two sides of a scale. Emotional intelligence is the fulcrum that balances this scale. Self-awareness helps us recognize when the scale is tipping too much to one side. If you're constantly working late, missing family dinners, or feeling drained, it's a sign that your work-life balance is off.

Emotional regulation provides us with the tools to restore this balance. It might involve setting boundaries at work, delegating tasks, or learning to say no. It could also mean carving out time for relaxation, hobbies, or social activities.

Achieving a healthy work-life balance reduces stress and enhances satisfaction in both work and personal life. As we navigate the tightrope of work and life, emotional intelligence serves as our balancing pole, ensuring we walk with stability, confidence, and grace.

12.4 TRIUMPH OVER MENTAL HEALTH CHALLENGES: AN EMOTIONAL INTELLIGENCE STORY

A Personal Tale of Overcoming Mental Health Challenges

Let's meet Thomas, a successful entrepreneur and loving father. Behind the backdrop of his accomplishment, however, was a battle with a formidable adversary—chronic anxiety. Despite his outward success, a sense of dread frequently plagued Thomas, a worry that something would go wrong and a fear that he wasn't good enough. These feelings started to creep into his professional life, impacting his decision-making skills and overall productivity. At home, his anxiety began to overshadow the joys of fatherhood, tainting his interactions with his children.

One day, during a particularly intense episode of anxiety, Thomas had a revelation. He realized that he couldn't let his anxiety rule his life. He sought help from a mental health professional and began his journey toward recovery.

The Role of Emotional Intelligence in Recovery

As part of his recovery, Thomas was introduced to the concept of emotional intelligence. He learned about self-awareness, emotional regulation, and empathy, and he began to see their potential in managing his anxiety.

He started practicing self-awareness, becoming more attuned to his feelings of anxiety. He learned to identify the triggers that worsened his anxiety, such as high-pressure situations at work or conflicts at home. This understanding gave him a sense of control over his anxiety, reducing its intensity.

Next, Thomas worked on emotional regulation. He learned techniques like deep breathing and progressive muscle relaxation, which helped him manage his physiological response to anxiety. He also practiced mindfulness, which helped him stay grounded in the present moment and prevented his mind from spiraling into worry.

Finally, Thomas learned about empathy. He started attending a support group for people with anxiety, where he could connect with others who shared similar experiences. He began to understand their emotions, and in doing so, he developed a better understanding of his own. This connection helped him feel less alone in his struggle, further reducing his anxiety.

Key Takeaways and Lessons Learned

Thomas's story sheds light on the transformative power of emotional intelligence in managing mental health challenges. Here are some key lessons from his experience:

1. Understanding Emotions Is Crucial: Recognizing and accepting our emotions is the first step toward managing them. By understanding his anxiety, Thomas was able to regain a sense of control over it, reducing its power over him.
2. Managing Emotions Is Powerful: Emotional regulation techniques can effectively manage anxiety, bringing about emotional balance. For Thomas, deep breathing, progressive muscle relaxation, and mindfulness were instrumental in managing his anxiety.
3. Understanding Others Helps Us Understand Ourselves: Empathy helps us understand others and provides insights into our own emotions. By connecting with others in his

support group, Thomas was able to better understand his anxiety and feel less alone in his struggle.

Thomas's transformation is a testament to the power of emotional intelligence in managing mental health challenges. His story offers hope to those facing similar struggles, affirming that with emotional intelligence, it is possible to navigate the stormy seas of anxiety and reach the shore of emotional balance and well-being.

As we turn the page to the next chapter, let's remember Thomas's story. It can inspire and guide us on our path toward mastering emotional intelligence.

CONCLUSION

As we close the final chapters of this insightful journey, it's important to reflect on what we've learned, its significance, and its potential for our future.

EMOTIONAL INTELLIGENCE: THE JOURNEY SO FAR

We embarked on a voyage of discovery, exploring the vast landscape of emotional intelligence. From understanding the fundamental pillars of emotional intelligence—self-awareness, emotional regulation, and empathy—to recognizing its profound influence on our personal growth, relationships, work, leadership, parenting, and mental health, our journey has been enlightening. We learned that emotional intelligence, often undervalued, holds the potential to enhance our lives in remarkable ways.

KEY TAKEAWAYS: THE EMOTIONAL INTELLIGENCE TOOLKIT

Our exploration has equipped us with valuable tools to navigate the complex world of emotions. We've learned to recognize and understand our emotions, manage our emotional responses, and empathize with others. We've delved into the transformative power of emotional intelligence in enhancing our relationships, achieving career success, nurturing our children, and managing mental health challenges. These tools form our emotional intelligence toolkit, ready to be used as we navigate the ups and downs of our lives.

THE FUTURE OF EMOTIONAL INTELLIGENCE: AN EXCITING PROSPECT

As we look ahead, the future of emotional intelligence is a field ripe with potential. Its relevance in our fast-paced, interconnected world is only set to increase. As we continue to navigate the complexities of our personal and professional lives, emotional intelligence skills will become increasingly vital. Knowing that we can enhance our lives by harnessing our emotional intelligence is an exciting prospect.

CALL TO ACTION: EMBRACE YOUR EMOTIONAL INTELLIGENCE JOURNEY

And so, I urge you, dear reader, to embrace your emotional intelligence journey. Take the tools you've gathered, the insights you've gleaned, and the wisdom you've acquired, and apply them in your life. Use them to enhance your relationships, excel in your work, nurture your children, and navigate your mental health. Remember, emotional intelligence is not a destination; it's a continuous journey. It's about striving, not for perfection, but for progress.

And as you continue your journey, remember you are not alone. I, too, am on this journey. As a passionate advocate for emotional intelligence, I've seen its transformative power, and I'm committed to sharing this knowledge to help others. I'm with you, cheering for you, and eager to see the positive changes that emotional intelligence will bring to your life.

Let's continue to learn, grow, and harness the power of our emotions. For in our emotional intelligence lies our strength, resilience, and ability to thrive in the complex tapestry of life. Let's embrace the journey, knowing that each step brings us closer to living a more fulfilling, emotionally intelligent life.

REFERENCES

Abdollahi, A., Abu Talib, M., & Motalebi, S. A. (2015, December 23). Emotional Intelligence and Depressive Symptoms as Predictors of Happiness Among Adolescents. https://doi.org/10.17795/ijpbs-2268

Cherry, K. (2023, December 31). 5 Key Emotional Intelligence Skills. VeryWellMind. https://www.verywellmind.com/components-of-emotional-intelligence-2795438

ChristineXP. (n.d.). How to Combat Overwhelming Emotions. Discovery Mood & Anxiety Program. https://discoverymood.com/blog/how-to-combat-overwhelming-emotions/

Cuncic, A., MA. (2024, February 12). 7 Active Listening Techniques For Better Communication. VeryWellMind. https://www.verywellmind.com/what-is-active-listening-3024343

David, S., & Congleton, C. (2013, November). Emotional Agility. Harvard Business Review. https://hbr.org/2013/11/emotional-agility

Denham, S. A., Zinsser, K., & Bailey, C. S. (2022, September). Emotional Intelligence in the First Five Years of Life. Encyclopedia of Early Child Development. https://www.child-encyclopedia.com/emotions/according-experts/emotional-intelligence-first-five-years-life

Druskat, V. U., & Wolff, S. B. (2001, March). Building the Emotional Intelligence of Groups. Harvard Business Review. https://hbr.org/2001/03/building-the-emotional-intelligence-of-groups

ESoft Skills Team. (n.d.). Strategies for Managing Workplace Stress With Emotional Intelligence. ESS Global Training Solutions. https://esoftskills.com/strategies-for-managing-workplace-stress-with-emotional-intelligence/

Farrahi, H., Kafi, S. M., Karimi, T., & Delazar, R. (2015, September 23). Emotional Intelligence and Its Relationship With General Health Among the Students of University of Guilan, Iran. https://doi.org/10.17795/ijpbs-1582

Göke, N. (2017, December 7). Emotional Agility Summary. Four Minute Books. https://fourminutebooks.com/emotional-agility-summary/

Gottman, J., Ph.D. (n.d.). Emotional Intelligence Creates Loving and Supportive Parenting. The Gottman Institute. https://www.gottman.com/blog/emotional-intelligence-creates-loving-supportive-parenting/

Guendelman, S., Medeiros, S., & Rampes, H. (2017, March 6). Mindfulness and

Emotion Regulation: Insights from Neurobiological, Psychological, and Clinical Studies. Frontiers in Psychology. https://doi.org/10.3389/fpsyg.2017.00220

Guy-Evans, O., MSc. (2023, September 29). The Difference Between Empathy And Sympathy. Simply Psychology. https://www.simplypsychology.org/sympathy-empathy-compassion.html

Hawthorne, R. (n.d.). 10 Techniques to Manage Anxiety and Increase Emotional Intelligence. Yoga Digest. https://yogadigest.com/10-techniques-to-manage-anxiety-and-increase-emotional-intelligence/

Intelligent Change. (n.d.). Emotional Intelligence and Its Role in Relationships. https://www.intelligentchange.com/blogs/read/emotional-intelligence-and-its-role-in-relationships

Little Reminders. (2023, July 7). From Chaos to Clarity: My Mindfulness Story. Medium. https://medium.com/@littlereminders.lr/from-chaos-to-clarity-my-mindfulness-story-6899bb61429c

Jiménez-Picón, N., Romero-Martín, M., Ponce-Blandón, J. A., Ramirez-Baena, L., Palomo-Lara, J. C., & Gómez-Salgado, J. (2021, May 18). The Relationship between Mindfulness and Emotional Intelligence as a Protective Factor for Healthcare Professionals: Systematic Review. National Library of Medicine. https://doi.org/10.3390/ijerph18105491

JM Official. (2024, September 4). Historical background and evolution of Emotional Intelligence. LinkedIn. https://www.linkedin.com/pulse/historical-background-evolution-emotional-intelligence-jm-official/

Klynn, B. (2021, June 22). Emotional regulation: Skills, exercises, and strategies. BetterUp. https://www.betterup.com/blog/emotional-regulation-skills

Korn Ferry. (n.d.). The Relationship between Emotional Intelligence and Leadership. https://www.kornferry.com/insights/featured-topics/leadership/relationship-between-emotional-intelligence-and-leadership

Malone, M. (n.d.). Emotional Intelligence in Relationships. Truity. https://www.truity.com/blog/page/emotional-intelligence-relationships

Mayo Clinic Staff. (n.d.). Resilience: Build skills to endure hardship. Mayo Clinic. https://www.mayoclinic.org/tests-procedures/resilience-training/in-depth/resilience/art-20046311

Miller, K., BA, CAPP. (2019, August 20). 50 Practical Examples of High Emotional Intelligence. PositivePsychology.com. https://positivepsychology.com/emotional-intelligence-examples/

Miller, L. (2022, July 1). Traditional vs. Emotionally Intelligent Parenting: 3 Ways EI Supports Parents and Children. EI Magazine. https://www.ei-magazine.com/post/traditional-vs-emotionally-intelligent-parenting-3-ways-ei-supports-parents-and-children

Moore, C. (2019, February 8). 19+ Innovative Ways to Teach Emotional

Intelligence to Kids. PositivePsychology.com. https://positivepsychology.com/emotional-intelligence-for-kids/

Morin, A., LCSW. (2023, May 9). How Cognitive Reframing Works. VeryWellMind. https://www.verywellmind.com/reframing-defined-2610419

Perficient Latin America. (2022, March 17). Emotional Intelligence: The Intelligence of Success. Perficient. https://blogs.perficient.com/2022/03/17/emotional-intelligence-the-intelligence-of-success/

Raypole, C. (2020, November 13). How to Identify and Manage Your Emotional Triggers. Healthline. https://www.healthline.com/health/mental-health/emotional-triggers

Riegel, D. G. (2019, January 30). 3 Emotionally Intelligent Strategies for Dealing with Difficult People. Inc. https://www.inc.com/deborah-grayson-riegel/difficult-person-driving-you-nuts-here-are-3-strategies-to-try-if-youve-tried-everything-else.html

Ringwald, W. R., & Wright, A. G. C. (2020, December 3). The Affiliative Role of Empathy in Everyday Interpersonal Interactions. NIH National Library of Medicine. https://doi.org/10.1002/per.2286

RocheMartin. (n.d.). Emotional Intelligence Case Studies. https://www.rochemartin.com/resources/case-studies

Roy Chowdhury, M. (2019, January 22). What Is Emotional Resilience? (+6 Proven Ways to Build It). PositivePsychology.com. https://positivepsychology.com/emotional-resilience/

Schueller, S. M., Neary, M., Lai, J., & Epstein, D. A. (2021, August 11). Understanding People's Use of and Perspectives on Mood-Tracking Apps: Thematic Analysis. National Library of Medicine. https://doi.org/10.2196/29368

Segal, J., Ph.D., Smith, M., M.A., Robinson, L., & Shubin, J. (n.d.). Improving Emotional Intelligence (EQ). HelpGuide.org. https://www.helpguide.org/articles/mental-health/emotional-intelligence-eq.htm

Seifert, C. (2020, March 6). The Case for Reading Fiction. Harvard Business Review. https://hbr.org/2020/03/the-case-for-reading-fiction

Singhal, M. (2021, January 3). 6 Things Emotionally Intelligent Parents Do Differently. Psychology Today. https://www.psychologytoday.com/us/blog/the-therapist-mommy/202101/6-things-emotionally-intelligent-parents-do-differently

Tanishisinghania. (2023, November 23). Emotional Intelligence in Practice: Stories from Real Life. Medium. https://medium.com/@tanishisinghania1/emotional-intelligence-in-practice-stories-from-real-life-2ad7a5b49d22

The Greater Good Science Center. (n.d.). What Is Mindfulness? University of California, Berkeley. https://greatergood.berkeley.edu/topic/mindfulness/defin

ition

Universal Class. (n.d.). The Impact of Emotional Intelligence and Personal Relationships. https://www.universalclass.com/articles/psychology/the-impact-of-emotional-intelligence-and-personal-relationships.htm

University of Rochester Medical Center. (n.d.). Journaling for Emotional Wellness—Health Encyclopedia. https://www.urmc.rochester.edu/encyclopedia/content.aspx?ContentID=4552&ContentTypeID=1

Urquijo, I., Extremera, N., & Azanza, G. (2019, November 29). The Contribution of Emotional Intelligence to Career Success: Beyond Personality Traits. NIH National Library of Medicine. https://doi.org/10.3390/ijerph16234809

Viezzer, S. (2023, October 9). IQ Vs EQ: Why Emotional Intelligence Matters More Than You Think. Simply Psychology. https://www.simplypsychology.org/iq-vs-eq.html

Zeng, G., Hou, H., & Peng, K. (2016, November 28). Effect of Growth Mindset on School Engagement and Psychological Well-Being of Chinese Primary and Middle School Students: The Mediating Role of Resilience. Frontiers in Psychology, 7. https://doi.org/10.3389/fpsyg.2016.01873

Made in the USA
Monee, IL
02 August 2024